Communicating with More Confidence

Rowmark

Other Easy Step by Step Guides in the series include:

Telemarketing, Cold Calling & Appointment Making

Marketing

Building a Positive Media Profile

Stress and Time Management

Motivating Your Staff

Recruiting the Right Staff

Better Budgeting for your Business

Writing Advertising Copy

Writing Articles and Newsletters

Managing Change

Handling Confrontation

Being Positive and Staying Positive

Giving Confident Presentations

Successful Selling

Communicating With More Confidence

Fundraising For Your School

Fewer, Shorter, Better Meetings

All the above guides are available from:

Rowmark Limited
65 Rogers Mead
Hayling Island
Hampshire
England PO11 0PL

Telephone: 023 9246 1931
Fax: 023 9246 0574
E mail: enquiries@rowmark.co.uk
www.rowmark.co.uk

Easy Step-by-Step Guide

Communicating with More Confidence

Pauline Rowson

Rowmark

Published by Rowmark Limited
65 Rogers Mead
Hayling Island
Hampshire
PO11 0PL

ISBN 0 9539856 9 5

Typeset by Freelance Publishing Services, Brinscall, Lancs
Printed in Great Britain by RPM Reprographics Ltd. Chichester.

This book is dedicated to my Dad

Joseph George Wilcox, a quiet man with a dry wit and a soft welsh accent who lost the power to speak and move in his last days of his illness but spoke volumes with his eyes.

Contents

About the author

Pauline Rowson lives in the UK and is a professional conference speaker who has helped countless individuals and businesses improve their communication skills. For over twenty years she worked in marketing, media and sales where she trained people in selling techniques, presentation skills and handling the media.

Her books include The Easy Step by Step Guides to *Successful Selling*; *Telemarketing, Cold Calling & Appointment Making*; *Building a Positive Media Profile*; *Marketing* and *Being Positive and Staying Positive*.

Introduction

Communicating effectively should be the simplest thing in the world, we talk and listen – or do we? And is that all there is to it? When things go wrong in a company, a friendship, a personal relationship, communication or rather lack of it or misinterpreting it, is often at the heart of the problem. Improving your communication skills can bring huge rewards; it can help you to win more contracts and sales, gain promotion, manage your organisation or your team more effectively, find friendship, even love. It can enhance relationships both at work and at home. So it's worth getting it right isn't it?

How to use this guide

This guide is written in as clear a style as possible to help you. I recommend that you read it through from beginning to end and then dip into it to refresh your memory. The boxes in each chapter contain tips to help you. Also at the end of each chapter is a handy summary of the points covered.

What you will learn from this guide

This book will provide tips and techniques to improve communication skills and gain the cooperation of others.

- how to read, interpret and use body language
- how to create the right visual appearance
- how to open, structure and close conversations
- how to influence people to your way of thinking
- how to persuade people to cooperate with you
- how to get on someone's wavelength
- how to recognise and relate to different personalities
- how to hear, recognise and use the different communication styles between men and women.

Note: to avoid confusion and the cumbersome use of 'he' or 'she' throughout the guide, 'he' has been adopted throughout. No prejudice is intended.

1

Anyone can communicate, can't they?

Of course they can. We can all communicate whether that is by speech, written word, sign language, Braille, body language, grunts, or simply the movement of the eyes if everything else is lost to us. Being able to communicate in some form is a great gift and one that we take for granted. If for some reason, medically or otherwise, we are robbed of the power to communicate then we would find it extremely frustrating and upsetting. Face to face communication is something to be treasured as is the power of speech and sight but are we losing the art of communicating or should I say communicating effectively? With more and more transactions being conducted by e-mail and text the need to talk face to face, or even on the telephone, is reducing. Many young people in particular are starting working life not knowing how to talk to their colleagues let alone customers and bosses, and many would rather use e-mail than pick up a telephone.

People are forgetting how to talk, how to listen and

how to pick up on subtle nuances of body language; this can lead to failed relationships and misunderstandings both in our social and our working lives.

Many people no longer know how to express themselves, what words to use and not to use. Worse still, they lack the confidence to meet other people or tackle difficult situations face-to-face, seeking to criticize, chastise and even worse dismiss people and end relationships by e-mail or text.

At work colleagues send e-mails to the person sitting at the desk next to them; managers instruct and inform by e-mail and then wonder why their instructions have been ignored or misinterpreted.

When things go wrong we often blame other people: if only they had expressed themselves more clearly, if only they hadn't assumed, if only they had listened to us. It is never our fault that we have failed to communicate effectively, is it? *Wrong*.

> We as individuals need to take full responsibility for communicating effectively. It is our responsibility, no one else's.

But why is this? Because you can never change another person. Many of us have tried and failed. Those that have succeeded haven't so much changed the other person they have changed themselves. By changing the way you think, behave, and react with others you can change the response you receive.

> You can only change you.

What is communication?

Given that we accept responsibility for communicating, we want to make it as successful as possible. Being able to communicate confidently means being able to achieve our desired goals without bullying others. However we communicate, whether it is through the spoken word, the written word or sign language it is for a purpose: to instruct or inform, to please, to entertain or to educate.

Face-to-face communication covers:

visually – how we look and our body language

vocally – how we speak

verbally – what we say

It also covers how we listen and how we think.

So there is another aspect to communication and an extremely important one and that is what we are thinking and feeling. This includes:

our inner voice

our level of self-confidence

our attitude, values, perceptions and prejudices

What makes a confident communicator?

Think for a moment of the people you believe to have been, or to be, confident communicators. These may be people you know either in your personal life or at work. They may be individuals you have heard speaking at a seminar or conference that you found inspirational. They may be people you have heard and seen on television, for example celebrities, personalities, and political leaders. Think about Winston Churchill and Martin Luther King both very powerful and confident communicators. What was it about these men that made them powerful communicators?

Exercise

Draw up a list of all the ingredients of a confident communicator. How many did you come up with?

Now look at my list below.

A confident communicator is someone who:

- knows his strengths and weaknesses
- has high self-esteem
- knows his subject matter
- has lots of energy, passion and enthusiasm (this doesn't mean to say he is hyperactive but communicates enthusiasm for his subject)
- has a clear voice
- is firm and persuasive
- uses words that his listener can relate to
- tailors his message to his audience
- has good body language
- has good listening skills
- has good questioning and summarising skills
- makes you feel valued, appreciated and comfortable
- has a sense of empathy with his listener

- has an open mind and is able to encourage a free flow of ideas
- gives a considered response when needed
- is able to build rapport and adapt his approach depending on who he is talking to.

You can already see from the above that it takes quite a lot to make a confident communicator. But practice makes perfect.

The benefits of confident communication

If the person who is communicating with you has all the above qualities how will you feel on the receiving end? Yes, valued and appreciated. This obviously has many benefits in the workplace. For example it can lead to:

- increased productivity
- better team working
- fewer mistakes and therefore more cost saving
- less stress
- less conflict
- fewer rumours
- better motivation
- greater profits
- a happier workforce.

The benefits of good communication in your personal

life can mean:

- fewer misunderstandings and therefore fewer rows
- greater cooperation
- more friends and an enhanced social life
- improved relationships

It's got to be worth giving it a go, hasn't it?

So if you've got this far and you want the rewards that come from being a more confident communicator, read on.

When confident communication can help

Communicating is at the heart of all good management. You cannot be an effective manager unless you know how to communicate confidently in whatever circumstances; this can be either on a one-to-one basis, with your team, or indeed if you are a senior manager or a director, to the entire organisation.

So confident communication is needed in all of the following situations:

- a one-to-one staff interview
- at an appraisal interview
- at a work review interview
- at a disciplinary interview
- at a counselling interview
- when dealing with a difficult member of staff
- when giving motivational feedback

- when giving a job interview
- when conducting a coaching interview
- when introducing changes and new policies at team meetings and briefings
- when giving presentations
- when handling customer complaints

If you are a salesperson you need confident communication in order to win the contract or sale.

If you are going for a promotion interview or a job interview you will need to communicate confidently in order to succeed.

If you are seeking to improve your relationships with your friends, family or partner you can do so through improving your communication skills.

How can you improve your communication skills?

You need to:

- ask the right questions
- listen effectively
- read and interpret body language
- understand what is being said behind the words
- use the right words

You need self-confidence, understanding and an open mind and you need to be unselfish, have a mature personality and be genuinely interested in other people.

In summary

- we must take full responsibility for communicating
- the only way to change or improve communication is to change the way you feel, think and act
- in order to communicate confidently you need to
  ask the right questions
  listen effectively
  read and interpret body language
  understand what is being said behind the words
  use the right words
- you also need:
  self-confidence;
  understanding;
  an open mind;
  an unselfish, mature personality;
  genuine interest in other people

2
Good communication starts within us

As I have already said confident communicators are self-confident people who have good self-esteem. They believe they are worth being listened to and they like to hear the views and opinions of others. They are able to both take and give criticism without feeling inadequate and hurt. They are assertive people who are able to express themselves without getting angry or upset and who encourage others to express their feelings and views.

If you have just read the above paragraph and are thinking 'That isn't me at all', then please don't despair and don't stop reading because you can develop self-confidence and improve your self-esteem, and you can adopt various techniques shown in this book to help you do this, and to convince others that you look more confident than you feel.

First though we need to understand all the influencing factors that come into play when we meet someone and how this affects our communication and ultimately the outcomes of that communication.

Exercise

Make a list of all the factors that you think influence you when making a decision about someone you meet for the first time.

How many did you come up with? Now compare your list with those below.

What influences us when we meet someone?

Appearance, which includes

clothes

adornments

body piercing and tattoos

hygiene – smell

clean/dirty

Body Language, which includes

eye contact

handshake

posture

facial expressions

Voice, which includes

accent

tone of voice

pitch and pace of voice

enthusiasm in the voice

Words: our vocabulary – the actual words we choose to use

Age

Size

Height

Gender

Race

Religion

Culture

Disability

Behaviour: yours and the other person's

manners

attitude

aggressiveness

submissiveness

assertiveness

Personality

Preconceived ideas about that person

Situation and location

Prejudices – yours and theirs

Education

Upbringing

Experiences

Status of the other person

It's quite a list, isn't it? And perhaps you came up with more! Looking at this is it no wonder we have 'communication breakdowns?' Perhaps you can also begin to see the logic of me saying that communication begins and ends with you.

In order to influence others you need to:

- plan how to interact with the other person
- have a greater awareness of other people
- be more sensitive towards their emotions and attitudes
- carefully observe other people
- have a greater self-knowledge

> **First impressions can often be the wrong impression**

When we meet someone we make a decision about that person within the space of milliseconds. That decision can be terribly flawed because it can be influenced by many of the factors previously stated.

How many times have you seen someone on your television, or heard them on the radio, and immediately thought 'That person really irritates me', or 'I don't like that person because he's got a beard and I don't like men with beards', (no offence intended towards men with beards) or

'Her voice really grates on me, I don't like her'.

You've never met this person and yet you have formed an opinion about them based on what you see and hear and your own preconceived ideas. The person you 'hate', or to put it less strongly, you 'dislike' may in fact be a very warm, kind, loving individual who, if you are given the opportunity to meet, you might actually like!

Politicians know the strength of this kind of reaction

and often they change the way they speak, look and behave in order to win votes. Margaret Thatcher, one time Prime Minister of Great Britain, lowered her voice and slowed down the pace of her speech to make her sound more authoritative and more caring. This is why actors sometimes make good politicians: because they are able to 'play the part' using their acting skills. These days votes aren't necessarily won on who has the best policies but who looks and sounds the best, or who appears the most sincere, trustworthy, honest ...

I am not advocating that politicians dupe people or that they, or you, set out to do the same just that you need to be fully aware of the power of **external** impressions on communicating an image.

What about the internal factors that influence us?

These internal factors, as I call them, are our:

- attitudes and perceptions
- values and pressures
- prejudices and preconceived ideas

Attitudes and perceptions

We need to be aware that the people we meet will come fully programmed with their own attitudes and their perceptions of us. Likewise we will have ours of them. This could, if not recognized and accepted, influence the exchange between us.

Poor managers often fail to recognize this. They tend to think that other people have the same attitude as them i.e. they are ambitious and want promotion. The manager may be motivated by reaching goals and receiving monetary rewards – isn't everyone? No, of course they're not, we are all different. Different people are motivated in different ways.*

So what forms our attitudes? Well, our exposure to previous experiences, information about that person, or even 'type of person', or the situation in which we are meeting them can all form our attitudes.

A very good example of this happened to me when some years ago I was running a training course in an hotel in southern England. The delegates arrived in the morning and I smiled and greeted them and tried to put them at their ease. It worked with most of the delegates except for two ladies, who completely blanked me out; they had very set expressions and were very hostile towards me. This isn't unusual because many trainers know that companies tell people they are being sent on a course without consulting them and without explaining why. It is the unfortunate trainer's task then to try and win this person round without alienating others. I thought this might have happened with the two ladies in question.

As we headed towards coffee break I noticed a thaw, they were beginning to participate and they were beginning to smile. I hadn't really done anything different but wondered if my 'open' approach had won them over.

At coffee break they came over to me and apologized for their somewhat hostile attitude towards me but they explained that they had been on a course the previous day, which according to them was 'terrible'.

---

*See The Easy Step-by-Step Guide, *Motivating Staff for Better Performance*

They were angry that they'd wasted their time, especially as they had come all the way from Scotland, some 500 miles. Because that other course had been so terrible they had 'assumed' they were going to have as bad a day as that with me. I am glad to say they didn't but it just goes to show how a previous experience can influence communication.

Another quite strange experience of mine also demonstrates this.

Years ago when I was much younger and working for the government I used to get a lift into work from a girl of my own age, which was then twenty-five. We were both married. We were friends and I worked with her and enjoyed her company. Then one day she said she could no longer give me a lift into work as it was too far out of her way. I was surprised but accepted her decision. Then she stopped talking to me. This was difficult because I worked with her. She became openly hostile and I could not work out what I had done wrong to cause this complete change in behaviour. In the end things got so bad that the boss called us in. She wanted to know what had happened to cause this rift in our relationship. I was absolutely dumbstruck when the other girl said that she had discovered her husband was having an affair and that the girl he was having an affair with looked very much like me! It wasn't me, but the fact that her husband's lover looked **like** me was enough!

Maybe she has never thought of it again, or can't remember the incident, but it is something that has stayed with me and reiterates how our experiences can shape our attitudes and the way we communicate with people.

Values

We all develop values, a frame of reference through which we see the world and the way things are. We love to categorize people, to think in stereotypes, because it helps us to place a value on ourselves and gives credence to the world in which we live. Of course, this stereotyping can, and often is, completely inaccurate and hence the way we communicate can be wrong from the start.

This can often be seen in industrial relations, the 'them' and 'us' scenario. Trade unions are greedy or bullying and management exploitative and selfish. In the so-called 'professions' lawyers, accountants and teachers are often referred to as 'professionals' while secretaries and clerks are often referred to as 'support staff'. Categorizing makes identification easier; if we know the other person's status then we know how to communicate with them, don't we? Wrong.

The more open-minded you can be when communicating with another person and the more you can see their viewpoint through their values (which may not be yours at all) the more you can understand them and perhaps engage the right tactics i.e. expressions, body language, voice, and vocabulary to relate to them.

Prejudices

We also inherit prejudices and beliefs from our parents, guardians, teachers, religious leaders, friends and many others. Perhaps we have been 'conditioned' not to like or understand people who are from a different culture? Perhaps we have been 'conditioned' to believe we are superior to others because of our education or social standing. Or we may be prejudiced towards someone because of his or her gender or his or her size. If this is so then we take those prejudices with us when we meet someone face-to-face and these prejudices can influence the whole exchange between us and that person and as a result we may be patronizing or hostile towards them.

It is hard to clear your mind of prejudices before meeting someone because instinctively, as I mentioned before, we try and place people in order to give us a framework for reacting with them, but that framework can be very wonky to begin with.

We are also influenced or conditioned by what we read and see in the media. Women are meant to behave in this way, men in that way, we should look tall, small, thin, beautiful and so on ... It is no wonder we're confused most of the time. Finding yourself and being comfortable with who you are is an important part of becoming a more confident communicator. I look at this in the next chapter.

Preconceived ideas

We may have preconceived ideas about the person we are communicating with because we have been told something about them. This has happened to me many times in the course of my career. I may be conducting a training course, giving a seminar or going to a meeting and someone has told me to look out for so and so because they are really difficult and hostile. This could colour my view of that person if I allowed it to. I might go into the meeting really worried about dealing with that person or thinking, 'I'll handle them, they won't get the better of me', and therefore act aggressively towards them before they have even had a chance to speak! Or I might be thinking, 'I hope they'll be all right. What if I can't handle them?' and therefore I might behave submissively, giving out a poor impression and allowing myself to be walked all over.

What usually happens is the 'difficult person' is no trouble at all. They are not difficult with me, not because they've suddenly changed overnight but because I have not allowed any preconceived ideas to interfere with the way I have communicated with them. I have kept an open mind and tried to listen to them and understand where they are coming from.

Sometimes the circumstances in which you meet someone, the location and/or the status of the person you are meeting will influence you. If a top movie star walked into the room how would you behave? If you were introduced to the Queen of England or the President of the United States of America would you be overawed? I would be and as a result I might burble away talking nonsense or I might completely clam up. That would be quite understandable in the circumstances. But sometimes it needn't be anyone that famous: it could be the boss of your company; it could be your mother-in-law, or father-in-law who you perceive to be, 'better' than you.

If you allow this thought process to continue unchecked then it will eat away at your confidence and affect how you feel towards them and ultimately how you behave and communicate towards them.

> No one is better than you. Everyone is different. Value your individuality.

Handling criticism

Criticism is always difficult to take no matter how pleasantly given and very often we can take it personally, especially if it is not given in a constructive manner or the person giving the criticism is not skilled in this, which, let's face it, few of us are. So how should we handle criticism if we are on the receiving end?

Let's take an example of the **mother-in-law who constantly criticizes her daughter-in-law.** She finds fault with her physical appearance, the way she manages the children, the food she cooks for her family, her housekeeping ability and so on, undermining her daughter-in-law's self-confidence until she dreads going anywhere near her mother-in-law. Her husband doesn't help as he lets the criticism go unchecked, causing friction in the marriage.

So let's try looking at this from a number of angles.

The daughter-in-law – we'll call her Carol – thinks the mother-in-law is a dragon, but instead of facing up to her and dealing confidently with the problem herself she attacks her husband, Michael, accusing him of being weak, uncaring and unloving towards her. Michael feels threatened by his wife's accusations, unhappy and torn between his mother and his wife and inadequate that he cannot face up to either, so he adopts the tactic of shrugging both off, believing that if he ignores the problem it will go away! Of course it doesn't: it only gets worse over the years.

So, before Carol plucks up courage to tackle her mother-in-law she needs to give some thought as to why her mother-in-law is behaving like this. What are her attitudes, values, pressures, thoughts and feelings?

Well she could be:

- jealous because she has lost her son to a rival
- resentful because Carol has taken her son away from her
- resentful because Carol and Michael have a better chance at happiness than she ever had
- jealous because Carol has more freedom than she had and more opportunities
- afraid – at being left on her own
- lonely
- frustrated because she has never fulfilled her own true potential
- disappointed – because she expected great things from her son and he has married too early and beneath her expectations (no matter how unrealistic).

So many things may be influencing the mother-in-law and these may have festered over the years and got blown up out of all proportion because she has never been able to express her emotions and communicate them effectively. If Carol can go into this exchange understanding or at least trying to see where her mother-in-law is coming from, or why she is behaving as she is, it will help her deal with it.

If you are on the receiving end of criticism from a relative or friend, like Carol, or from someone at work, then first consider that the other person has a right to criticize you. If you do not do this then you will behave aggressively. If Carol is thinking 'What right has my mother-in-law got to criticize me?' then she will behave aggressively towards her mother-in-law.

However, if you accept they have the right to criticize you then you will also want them to accept that you have rights. The right not to be put down, not to be made to look small or to be subjected to personal attacks; also that you have a right for that criticism to be made in private rather than in front of colleagues or others. Here are some tips to help you deal with this.

> If you are unclear about the meaning of the criticism then ask the other person for clarification.

I find this particularly helpful because asking them what they mean gives me time to get the right mindset and to think of my reply. It also means they have to repeat themselves and people rarely say the same thing twice. Say something like, 'I'd find it helpful, Mary, if you could give me some examples of what you mean.' **Not** 'What the devil do you mean by that!' (More about this in Chapter 10.)

Try and separate in your mind the content of the criticism and the way it is given. If this has happened before, say, 'I accept that your criticism is valid, Laura, but I'd prefer it if you made it less of a personal attack.'

If you disagree with the criticism then say so. Again use the 'I' statement, 'As I see it, that is not what happened' or 'My view is different.' This is a technique that Carol should adopt with her mother-in-law. (See Chapter 9 and Chapter 13 for more on this.)

Maintain steady eye contact. Keep your voice up,

rather than letting it sink, but don't get high-pitched, 'I don't believe *that!'*

Giving constructive criticism

If you need to give criticism then check it is specific and not a personal attack.

'Chris, I've noticed your sales figures have been low these last two months why is that?'

Not, *'Chris, you'd better pull your socks up and get some more sales otherwise it'll be curtains for you.'*

Don't jump to conclusions; they might be the wrong ones. Chris's sales figures might be low because he has personal problems or ill health. The **why** question is vital here and we look at questioning techniques in more detail in Chapter 8.

Give the other person the chance to reflect on it and state his case. You can then go on to ask for suggestions to bring about desired change, for example, *'What are your ideas for improving this?'*

Handling criticism in a personal relationship

Women, generally speaking, are much more vocal about their criticism than men when it comes to personal relationships. This has its roots in the fact that women like to voice their feelings and emotions, preferring to get them out into the open and discuss them whereas men prefer to retreat into themselves, into their 'cave'. When a man refuses to discuss a problem or respond to a criticism he can often be accused by a woman of trying to wriggle out of it.

In a healthy relationship both men and women should be able to express their criticisms openly, without fear or anger or upsetting the other person, but all too often, in the heat of the moment, criticism when it comes can be construed as a personal attack. This leaves the person on the receiving end feeling bitter, angry, hurt and upset. If the criticism is also given in a hostile or bitter tone of voice, and/or is accompanied by a look of contempt or loathing, then the person on the receiving end is going to be deeply wounded. If this forms a continual pattern over a period of time then the danger signs are that one partner has made a judgement about the other for the worse which can result in that partner either fighting back (sparks will fly) or stonewalling, (generally a man's response), retreating into silence. This in turn can lead to the eventual break-up of the relationship.

One partner in this relationship will begin to feel that he or she is the innocent victim of the criticism and that the other person is always picking on them, which can result in that person experiencing a feeling of righteous indignation – 'how dare he/she?'- fuelling anger. Once these thoughts become an automatic response they are self-confirming: the partner who feels victimized will be scanning everything for some hidden slight to confirm the view, thereby poisoning the relationship until the break-up.

But it needn't get this far if we can learn to handle criticism in a healthy way. Having an inner confidence and good self-esteem can help (see Chapter 3) but also when you feel inclined to criticize your partner, before you do so stop and think.

For men, when your partner/wife criticizes you don't

side-step it or stonewall it but look upon it as a way of improving the relationship. It is not a personal attack but a means of saying 'what do we need to do/change to make this situation/ relationship better?' Listen to her and empathize, don't rush in to solve the problem.

And for women, examine the nature of your criticism and make it less of a personal attack and more a constructive criticism over what was done, the action or activity rather than the person.

For both, before criticizing or being irritated by what the other person has done or said counteract this with the good things about that person: recall their generosity, kindness, loving, thoughtfulness, fun etc.

Fundamental to successful communication is the ability to understand others. Being able to enter into their inner world, see things from their frame of reference and agree its validity from their perspective.

We cannot communicate more confidently without looking first at ourselves.

In summary

- confident communicators are:

  self-confident people who have good self-esteem;

  people who believe they are worth being listened to;

  people who like to hear the views and opinions of others;

  able to both take and give criticism without feeling inadequate and hurt;

  assertive people who are able to express

themselves without getting angry or upset;

people who encourage others to express their feelings and views.

- many factors influence you when you meet someone, so you need to:

  plan how to interact with the other person;

  have a greater awareness of other people;

  be more sensitive towards their emotions and attitudes;

  carefully observe other people;

  have a greater self-knowledge

- the factors that have a powerful influence on the way we communicate are our

  attitudes and perceptions;

  values and pressures;

  prejudices and preconceived ideas

- we all think our own limited view is the real one. It is not
- fundamental to successful communication is the ability to understand others
- we cannot communicate more confidently without looking first at ourselves.

3

Building confidence

> Acting more confidently begins with thinking more confidently.

Your brain is a very powerful organ, it sends messages to your body, and those messages are relayed to other people through your body language i.e. how you walk, sit, stand, your facial expressions and eye contact etc. Therefore, if you think that your point of view is useless and that nobody will be interested in listening to you, if you feel afraid, or you see yourself as inferior then this will be relayed to other people through your body language and, because those are the signals they are receiving, they in turn will view you in exactly that light. It is a vicious circle that you need to break and one which you *can* break.

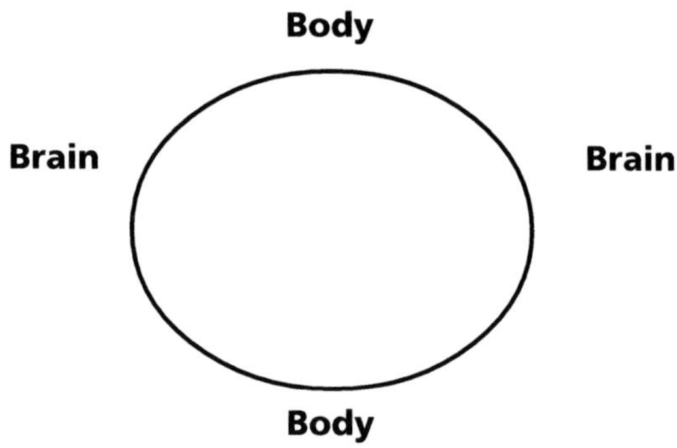

> If you can learn to think more highly of yourself then others will think more highly of you.

What is self-esteem?

Self-esteem is the picture we have of ourselves and the value we place upon ourselves. It is dependent on what others tell us about ourselves either directly or indirectly by the way they treat us.

For example if you have continually been told as a child that you are too clumsy, too fat, too tall, or hopeless at school this could very well be the picture that you end up forming of yourself. If you are told you are useless you may come to believe that you are useless.

Here's an example.

Tim is seven years old. He has made a new friend at school and his teacher has praised him for some work that he did. As a result he was awarded his first gold star. He is bursting with pride and full of enthusiasm.

He rushes out of the school gate to tell you but you've had a bad day, you're late for an appointment, you haven't got time to listen to him. How do you think Tim will feel? Yes, like he's been slapped in the face.

Then Tim has another chance to repeat his wonderful news when his father returns home from work. But his father is too tired; he's had a row with the boss. He's worried about being made redundant and he tells Tim to be quiet, or go to bed. Again how do you think Tim will feel? You've got it, bitterly disappointed. If this pattern is repeated and continues what these parents are telling Tim is that he is not worth listening to. His experiences are of no consequence to them so Tim begins to feel worthless. His self-esteem has suffered a severe blow, which could then affect the rest of his schooling and indeed his life.

Research has shown that feelings of inadequacy start very young, from birth in fact and are clearly apparent by the time a child reaches the age of ten.

Teachers, parents, guardians all signal to children that they value them as individuals. They do this by listening to them, by setting realistic standards, by encouraging them not to be daunted by failure, by urging them to have the confidence to try again and to act independently and responsibly.

Girls generally have lower self-esteem than boys even in the western world and this is largely due to the cultural and general status of women in society. When girls are paired with boys to perform a task, girls can artificially depress their performance so as not to outshine the boys.

This can also happen in the workplace. Women very often compensate for their lower feelings of self-esteem by over planning and they don't always realize they are doing this. Women also tend to worry more about the task and attend to it more thoroughly, in order to prove they are as good as the men.

In addition, many women set themselves lower goals in life. They are more inclined to undervalue their abilities. If a woman is praised for a project, or a particular aspect of her work, she is much more likely than a man to say 'Oh it was nothing', simply shrugging it off and getting embarrassed while a man is more comfortable at accepting the praise even acknowledging and confirming it by saying, 'Yeah, I did well there.' Sometimes he will even bring it to the attention of the boss himself seeking out the praise.

In order to counterbalance this and boost self-esteem in girls and women they need to be encouraged to be more adventurous, to take risks. Indeed everyone should be told that to fail is not the end of the world but the road to improvement. We can learn a great deal more from our failures and grow from them than we can from our successes and yet in many cultures failure is not to be countenanced.

How can we improve our self-esteem?

Many of us have been raised that to think or say nice things about ourselves is not 'right'. It is sometimes much easier for us to find fault with ourselves than to find the 'good' in ourselves. It's all very well to be self-deprecating but this can become a habit, and a bad one at that. If we are always putting ourselves down then how can we ever communicate confidently?

So let's try the following exercise:

Exercise

Taking a piece of paper write down the following:

1 Two physical attributes you like about yourself

2 Two personality qualities you like about yourself

3 One talent or skill that you like in yourself.

How easy was that for you? If you found it difficult, which many people do, then find someone whose opinion you value and trust and ask them to complete it for you, (you can also do the same for them) and then exchange notes. This can be a great confidence boosting exercise.

Next keep this piece of paper with you, to refresh yourself of your good points particularly when feeling low or nervous.

If you constantly focus on the negative then you will give out negative thoughts, your body language will give out the same and not only will you continue to feel negative but others will react to you in a negative or hostile way, or they will completely dismiss you and your opinions.

So you need to constantly remind yourself of your good qualities and what you have got going for you. Retrain your brain into thinking about the positive and not the negative. Your body language will therefore change and you will start to give out more positive body language signals.

> Feel good about yourself – also learn to feel good about others

Sometimes we are so self-absorbed that we become inward looking and selfish, wanting what we want, when we want it and how we want it. We think we are the only ones suffering, or the only ones that matter, the only ones who have any problems. We become obsessed about how we feel and some people thrive on the attention this brings them feeding their inner vanity so that they become even more self-obsessed.

> **Learning to think of others and yourself in a positive way can be the first step towards an inner confidence.**

You can gain a great deal of personal satisfaction and strength through helping others.

Figure out what is important to you and let go of the rest - there isn't time for everything. Take a moment to think how you would like to be remembered when you are gone. Are you living that life? If not, why not? What can you do to change it? You have the power to create your own dreams and use your experiences to help as many people as you can. By giving out you can take the focus off yourself and find greater inner confidence and gain self-esteem.

Your inner voice

Let's look at what else stands in your way - your inner voice. What is it saying to you? Is it a positive one or a negative one?

For example, you might be saying: *'It's all right for her, she had a good education, of course she is more confident than me.'*

Or

'He's only got to the top because he sucked up to the boss', or *'... his father owns the company'*, or *'... he's cleverer than I am'*.

The above are faulty inner dialogues – they are hostile and embittered and focus on you. If you don't correct them then they **will** affect your body language and therefore the signals you are giving out to other people so that in turn you behave aggressively; i.e. you look, move and sound surly, or bitter, your expression is hard and resentful, you may make cryptic remarks and snide comments. Is this the sort of person you want to be? How do you think others will react to you? Would you want to be around a person like this and would you be willing to do as they asked? I doubt it.

Or instead of getting aggressive you may become submissive. If you are constantly comparing yourself to others and you are coming off the worse, you are constantly putting yourself down. Or you may be allowing yourself to wallow in self-pity. Your self-esteem will be low and your body language will be become hunched and withdrawn. You want to fade into the background and not be noticed. Will you take the initiative and forge new relationships? Will other people be inspired to cooperate with you? Of course they won't.

You may be dealing with someone who is rude or difficult and your inner dialogue may be saying something like, *'I wish that person wasn't so difficult, they're a right pain in the ...' 'I can't stand that person. I wish they would see my point of view, or act like me.'*

When you hear these negative, prejudiced voices say **STOP.** Then get a more positive dialogue going. Here are some to help you:

I have an open mind.

I will treat this person fairly.

I can keep calm.

I am interested in this person and what they have to say.

I may not agree with this person but he/she has a right to his/her point of view.

I may not like this person but I can treat him decently and fairly.

If any of these phrases are going through your head what signals do you think your body language is giving out?

Yes, you will be looking at the other person, giving them good eye contact. Your facial expression will be relaxed and interested. You may even have your head on one side as you listen to them. Your posture will be upright, but not stiff, open and relaxed, you may even be leaning more towards the other person, to show interest.

Remember Carol and her mother-in-law in the previous chapter? If Carol is saying to herself, *'I really dislike my mother-in-law, I find her so unreasonable and difficult to deal with. I dread going to see her'*, then she is **programming** herself to react to her mother-in-law in a **negative** way. Her brain will send negative messages to her body language, which in turn will be aggressive. Mother-in-law will see Carol as bad-tempered, irritable, surly, uncooperative etc, fulfilling her own prophecies of her daughter-in-law.

Carol can't change her mother-in-law but she can change herself. She can choose to say instead,

'My mother-in-law has a reason for behaving the way she is. I feel sorry for her that she feels she has to make these remarks. I will try to understand her and like her.'

Try smiling at a difficult person, genuinely smiling; try saying something nice to them instead of getting upset or hostile. Think of **them** rather than focusing on what hurts and upsets you. Take your difficult person by surprise by complimenting them. I am not promising that it will work every time but it will make you feel better.

> Remember: you cannot change another person; you can only change yourself. By changing the way you think, act and interact with others you will change the response you receive in return.

Thinking more confidently may take some time and indeed some practice but it will help you to communicate more confidently.

In summary

- acting more confidently begins with thinking more confidently
- if you think more confidently you will get people to cooperate with you more easily

- you cannot change another person; you can only change yourself
- be aware that what you are thinking about a person will show through in your body language
- take stock of yourself and your good points and keep reminding yourself what they are.

4

Your appearance – clothes and grooming

Most of us are familiar with makeover programmes on the television and articles in magazines where a man or a woman is given a new look. Often the results can be quite startling and the individual feels elated. We all get stuck in a rut, buying familiar styles and colours that we feel comfortable with. There is nothing wrong with this but from time to time it does us good to reassess ourselves and to consider the impression we're giving out to others; is it the right impression?

If we try and wear the same clothes at forty as we did at sixteen (if they still fit us) how do you think that would look? Yes, pretty foolish I think. The way to feel and look younger is not to embrace the latest fashion fads, nor to stick with those tired old clothes we found so invigorating when young but to reassess our appearance as we get older and find styles, colours and clothes that suit us and can reflect our personalities; clothes that are timeless and stylish and of the best quality we can afford and hence give us a boost in confidence.

Over the years our skin tone changes, so too does our hair colour. Our shape alters and because of these changes our clothes, make up, hairstyle all need to change.

By changing clothes, hairstyle etc. you can feel completely different, often rejuvenated and your body language and communication style will therefore also change. You feel, look and act differently. People will then respond to you differently.

Research conducted by Professor Albert Mehrabian, a psychologist, showed that our decisions about the people we meet are based on the following:

55 per cent	what we see
38 per cent	what we hear
7 per cent	the words we are speaking

We're going to take each of these in turn, examine them and see how we can use them to communicate a more confident image. But first what we see – our appearance.

Clothes

> **People will form an impression of you based on what you are wearing.**

Of course that sounds extremely shallow and it is. That impression may be completely wrong but whether you like it or not it is a fact of life that your appearance says a great deal about you.

But it is no good creating a false impression, the one

you project needs to reflect who you are and what you are capable of. You need to be comfortable with your image and that only comes with being comfortable with who you are inside, which we examined in Chapter 2.

If you choose to mirror someone else's image or style, a well known singer or celebrity for example, then you are bound to be disappointed because you can never be like them. You are a different person with a different shape, style and personality.

You are *you* and you need to be proud of that and confident in yourself to project it.

If you choose to dress 'outrageously' then that is your choice, however you must be prepared for reactions you may get from others, which could vary from hilarity to alienation.

We all have our 'uniforms', suits for the office, green Wellingtons, Barbours and checked shirts for the country, designer clothes, leathers for the motorbike riders. Some of these uniforms are donned because they are practical. You wouldn't wear an evening suit on a country walk, would you? But uniforms also have another purpose, they show you belong and belonging to a group is part of a human need. By dressing outside that group's norm you are signalling that you don't belong and can therefore feel and indeed be isolated. I am sure most of you reading this book can identify a time when you wore the wrong clothes to a function and felt awful and out of place. Perhaps you were too casually dressed for the occasion, or overdressed.

I remember attending a very high society wedding once where my husband and I donned a buttonhole because this was the 'norm' at all the previous weddings we'd attended. When we arrived at the wedding we noticed that not one single person was sporting a carnation and indeed we drew some very peculiar looks. We seemed to have committed a social faux pas. Surreptitiously my husband and I withdrew behind a stone pillar and quickly whipped the carnations from our buttonholes.

Clothes also affect the way we feel and therefore our body language. For example you move very differently if dressed in glamorous evening attire as opposed to a tracksuit, or in a suit as opposed to jeans.

If your clothes are old, worn, tatty and dirty, what impression is that giving out? What is this saying to others? How does it make you feel?

If your clothes are clean and tidy what impression are you projecting? How do you feel? You may not be able to afford the top quality designer wear or the most expensive clothes, but there is no excuse for looking dirty or scruffy, as my dear late father-in-law used to say and he had very little money and used to buy his clothes from charity shops. You can find some great bargains in charity shops and at the same time know you are helping a worthwhile cause. So you don't need a fortune in order to look good.

You can also do wonders with a needle and sewing machine or with knitting needles; you can make the latest designer fashions very cheaply. I am both an amateur dressmaker and knitter, not a very good one, but practice makes perfect and it is a very enjoyable and rewarding pastime. You can make children's clothes very cheaply as well as your own and you can look good and individual.

If your clothes are rather on the old side because perhaps you can't afford new ones then maybe you can update them slightly (with that needle and thread) or you can take them to a dressmaker or tailor who can update them for you.

Whatever you do, do ensure that your clothes are clean and well pressed. Try not to wear shirts with frayed necks and cuffs unless you really don't care what impression you give out, or you have the inner confidence and personality to carry it off.

Different nationalities have their own 'uniform' and customs, be aware of this and don't let it prejudice the way you communicate.

Giving some careful consideration to the impression you wish to convey and the objectives you wish to achieve can help you to choose the right clothes.

This is a quote taken from my local newspaper from a woman who was interested in meeting a partner and was going to local pubs, and social functions with that aim.

'I spoke to a couple of men but because I was wearing quite a low cut top they spent time talking to my cleavage rather than to me!'

Well there's a surprise! If this woman was really serious about meeting someone she could have a conversation with, and who was interested in her as a person then perhaps she shouldn't have had so much cleavage on view?

At work the general rule for women in the western business world is: the more flesh you show the less credible you are. If you arrive at the office dressed for the disco, in the tightest, skimpiest clothes you can find then how do you think the hot-blooded men around you are going to react?

Of course they are. That may be your intended desire to inflame some passions but make sure you don't get your fingers burnt. I've lost count of the number of times women have said to me in my career, *'Why aren't I taken seriously?'* I've simply told them to take a long hard look in the mirror at what they're wearing to the office and think about the effect it has on their male colleagues.

And what about men in the workplace? Well they've got their suit, haven't they? But times have changed and are changing. There are now many more dress options for men going to work from the smart to the smart casual and casual-casual. Just how casual do you dress on a Friday dress down day? That interview you are attending – what is the dress code of that particular company? Will you be overdressed in a suit and tie when everyone wears open necked shirts and chinos? Do you wear coloured shirts or a white shirt? I once did some work for a company where the Managing Director told me he wouldn't employ anyone wearing a coloured shirt!

Before attending an interview perhaps it would be advisable to telephone the company and ask if they have a dress code and what it is.

If you aspire to a management position then you should always dress the part. In fact you should always dress for the next level up and not the level you currently hold if you wish to be noticed and considered. This does not always mean adopting a formal style of dressing because it depends on the industry you are working in and the 'uniform' or 'dress code' within that industry.

Do make sure your shoes are clean and that goes for both men and women. I have sat in on a number of sales presentations, promotion and job interviews when a candidate has ruined his/her overall impression by having dirty or scuffed, shoddy shoes. This can be all it takes to cause you to fail. Interviews can be nerve racking and difficult as it is without adding to it by neglecting your appearance.

Choosing what to wear to work, for a sales presentation or job interview can sometimes be a difficult choice, particularly so for women who have more scope for error than men because they have more choice.

So ask yourself:

Where am I going?

Why am I going there?

What is the normal dress code or uniform for that occasion or group of people?

What impression do I wish to project?

What should I wear?

Colour

The colour of your clothes can have a considerable impact on how you are perceived. If you visit your local supermarket and look at the products on the shelves, think about the colour of the packaging. Why has that company chosen blue, or green or red? What is the message that colour projects? Why do we choose different colours to decorate our homes? The psychology of colour also comes into play with our clothes. Not only does it have an impact on how we are perceived but also how we feel.

Have some fun with word associations – throw out a colour to a group of people and ask them for their immediate reaction to that colour and see what you get back. There may be some very common associations.

Different colours often have different meanings in different cultures, so be aware of this when visiting overseas or doing business abroad.

Whatever colours you choose to wear they should suit you and not drain you: here you might wish to take some expert advice. It could save you a great deal of money in the long run as you no longer waste it on buying clothes that you don't like once you get them home from the shop.

Let's look at some colours and see what they mean.

Black

In the western world black signifies formal, authority, sober but that isn't all it means. It is often worn at funerals and old-fashioned villains and witches wore black. Priests wear black to signal submission to God and some fashion experts say that black worn by a woman signifies submission to men! But many women like black because they believe it makes them look slimmer. However, because it is such a heavy colour and absorbs light, it has the opposite effect on someone who is not already slim, overpowering them and making them appear bigger and heavier and therefore making others feel rather nervous around them.

We also tend to think black is sophisticated and glamorous. It can be, but only if it suits you. Not everyone looks good in black - in fact I look like death warmed up - it drains me both physically and mentally. Men in black suits, or black pin-striped suits set off by a white shirt, can look quite stunning but they are also giving out an authoritative air. Waiters wear black and white to show they have authority on the restaurant floor and so that they can be recognized as waiters. A smartly turned out waiter or waitress in black and white can add serenity and sobriety not to mention class to a restaurant. But if you are a woman attending an interview and you decide to wear a black suit with a white blouse then beware, it is unlikely you will get the job. Why? Because black and white can be overpowering, aloof and hostile and can therefore threaten the interviewer. If the only suit you own is black and the only blouse white then try and break the harshness of this combination of colours by adding a coloured scarf, or for men set it off with a coloured tie. Accessories are a lot cheaper than buying a whole new suit.

Red

Red signifies energy and physical strength. It also signifies aggression and danger: fire engines are red. I remember reading somewhere that red cars are involved in more accidents than any other colour yet red cars are popular. Why? Because red also symbolizes power. It is an intense colour and often makes the wearer (or user) feel more confident. I once had a red skirt that I loved wearing. But again another word of warning: if you choose to wear red then also choose where and when to wear this colour. If you are a woman and you choose to wear a red jacket to work you may find this doesn't help you in a meeting with your male colleagues. Because it is a power colour it may say that you are trying to exert your power over your male colleagues too much. If you are the boss then fine, but if not you may find yourself being isolated or attracting aggression. Men don't wear red jackets unless they work for Butlins, the holiday and entertainment company. However, men can wear red ties and this will have the same effect as the woman wearing the red jacket. You may recall in the 1980s that the smart 'yuppie' - the man on the up – was seen sporting red braces! If you are involved in negotiations or conflict situations red might not be the most appropriate colour to choose as it signals aggressiveness and your aim might be to gain cooperation.

Pink

Pink is a more tranquillising colour, soothing and feminine. All the pastel colours of pink, blue, and lilac symbolize tranquillity and femininity. So you are back to deciding who you are seeing and the impression you wish to project. What is the aim of your meeting? If you need to project authority and energy, or perhaps gain promotion or get that job, dressing yourself in pastel colours may not be communicating a very confident and assertive image and this also applies to men wearing pastel coloured shirts and ties.

Green

Green is the colour of nature. It is a calming colour but too much green can communicate we are lazy, too relaxed. It is not a very assertive colour especially when it becomes a muddy green, which moves towards signifying death. Green is also associated with envy, resentment and possessiveness. Some people hold that it is a colour of bad luck and they will not wear it or have it in the house, my mother is one such person, although personally I like it in the home but cannot wear it, as it does not suit me. In the middle ages, brides wore green as a symbol of fertility.

Yellow

This is a bright, sunny, optimistic colour. It is associated with the intellectual side of the mind giving out the impression of someone who is clear thinking, has good judgement and able to make decisions. However too much yellow can be overpowering. Yellow can help to build self-confidence, it enhances the concentration and conveys a good organizer but beware of a muddy yellow, which can signify liverishness.

Blue

Blue inspires mental control and clarity. It is also associated with creativity. It is the colour of the sky and ocean. It is peaceful and tranquil but can be cold and aloof. Blue is often a good colour to wear to an interview as it symbolizes loyalty and productivity. Studies show that weightlifters are able to lift heavier weights in blue gyms. Too much dark blue however can be depressing.

Turquoise

Turquoise is invigorating. It refreshes us, lifts us and is good for stimulating communication, sensitivity and creativity. Funnily enough I often wear turquoise when writing my crime novels.

Brown

Brown is a solid reliable colour, it is the colour of the earth, bringing with it stability. It can also be sad and wistful and can imply narrowmindedness and retreat. Men tend to like brown.

Grey

Grey tends to have a negative feeling, as it is associated with poor weather, grey clouds, grey sky, heavy and dull. It is neither black nor white, the colour therefore of evasion, giving the impression of lack of commitment and loneliness.

By now you're probably trawling through your wardrobe in despair wondering what colours you can possibly wear! Well, you should:

- wear the colours that suit you and enhance your complexion, not the ones that drain you.
- wear the colours that make you feel comfortable and confident
- choose which colours to wear when and on what occasion.

Attending an interview

When attending an interview try to avoid extremes of fashion, no tight or revealing clothing, no strong perfume or aftershave or large jewellery that jangles every time you move - and don't forget to check those shoes.

Use clothes to assert yourself, choosing the clothes that make you feel confident and that suit you. Be aware of your body shape and clothes that emphasize this or hide it. Learn to play up your strengths and down your weaknesses. Look at buying good accessories.

Trousers should not be too long and hanging over shoes. Neither should they be flying at half-mast, displaying Mickey Mouse socks or, worse, white socks. Shoes in both men and women should match the colour of the trousers: brown shoes should not be worn with a dark suit, navy, black or grey trousers. In women, shoes should be the same colour or darker than a skirt, and tights or stockings should also be darker than or of the same colour as the skirt.

Whether male or female, if you are wearing trousers that have belt loops then do wear a matching belt. Again, ensure that your trousers sit comfortably on you and that they are not torn in any way. Yes, I have seen a man with trousers torn at the crutch!!

Make sure your clothes fit you and that your shirt or blouse is not straining across your midriff. Also, if wearing a jacket, make sure it fits when fastened. (There is more on interviews in Chapter 6).

Giving a presentation

If you are giving a presentation then think of your audience. Adapt your outfit to tone in with your audience. If I am giving a talk to a group of educationalists then I will dress smartly but more informally. I will wear neutral colours that look and feel comfortable and do not threaten the audience. I often wear white blouses, t-shirts and jumpers not only because white happens to suit me but it also reflects honesty. White itself is a neutral colour and therefore not particularly threatening unless you associate it with 'the men in white coats' coming to take you away, ha, ha! It can, though, sometimes be a bit overpowering and I will often soften my white with a coloured scarf.

If I am giving a conference talk to a group of bankers, lawyers or accountants I will always wear a suit, usually navy blue to aid authority. Try not to choose overpowering colours or clothes as that will only overpower your message. You want people to remember you and what you talked about, not what you wore.

Research your audience and adapt your outfit to tone with your audience's style. If your audience, however, are going to be casually dressed do not tone down your attire completely by wearing jeans and a t-shirt. You need to maintain some authority so you should be dressed casually but smartly.

> Never let your appearance overpower your message.

Beware of clothes with bold patterns, and avoid dangling earrings or bracelets that jangle, which will be extremely irritating for the audience, as irritating as a man turning over the loose change in his pocket! (There is more on giving presentations in Chapter 6.)

Good grooming is essential

In all cases whether it is for an interview, promotion, presentation, at work or out to impress someone on a date good grooming is essential. Hair and nails should be clean and no chipped nail varnish, ladies.

Check your breath. A good way to know if you suffer from bad breath is to lick the inside of your wrist, wait for five seconds then sniff it. This will tell you. Or visit a dentist and ask his professional advice. Having bad breath, like having bad body odour, is something even your best friends won't tell you. It is so personal and yet something can be done about both.

Make up

For women make up can enhance promotion and job prospects. Even if you hate wearing make up then at least try wearing lipstick. Lipstick enables a woman's face to look finished and well groomed. It projects power and confidence. Powerful women through history have always understood the significance of wearing make up, especially lipstick, from Cleopatra to Queen Elizabeth I, Margaret Thatcher and Hilary Clinton. And yet some women can't wear it because of religious or cultural reasons, or choose not to wear it because they simply don't like it, or it doesn't fit with their personal beliefs. That is fine, it isn't the end of the world, it won't cause you to fail as long as the rest of your appearance is clean and tidy and your appearance is well groomed.

And finally ...

At work women should carry an extra pair of tights or stockings and men a tie, in case of accidents.

If the baby has been sick on your nice clean suit or shirt before leaving for the office make sure you can sponge it off in the toilets at work if you haven't got time to change.

In summary

- from time to time it does us good to reassess our image: is it the image we want to project or is it out of date?
- the way to feel and look younger is not to embrace the latest fashion fads, nor to stick with those tired old clothes you found so invigorating when young but to reassess your appearance
- buy clothes that reflect your personality, that are timeless and stylish and of the best quality you can afford
- by changing clothes, hairstyle etc. you can feel completely different, often rejuvenated and your body language and communication style will therefore also change
- you need to be comfortable with your image and that only comes with being comfortable with who you are
- clothes also affect the way we feel and therefore our body language
- the general rule for women in the western business world is, the more flesh you show the less credible you are
- if you aspire to a management position then you should always dress the part or the next level up
- when choosing what to wear ask

  Where am I going?

  Why am I going there?

  What is the normal dress code or uniform for that occasion or group of people?

What impression do I wish to project?

- the colour of your clothes can have a considerable impact on how you are perceived
- use clothes to assert yourself, choosing the clothes that make you feel confident and that suit and fit you.

5

Body language – greetings and introductions

> You never get a second chance to make a first impression.

The first impression you make can also be a lasting impression. Therefore you need to make sure you get that first impression right.

Having decided what you should wear and how you should look to help you to communicate a more confident image, you also need to be aware of the body language signals you are giving out.

Body language includes:

- eye contact and eye movement
- distance from others e.g. personal space zone
- posture and stance

- facial expressions
- gestures

Non verbal signals you give out (i.e. body language signals) are said to be four and a half times more powerful than your verbal signals.

Your facial expression is at least eight times more powerful than the spoken word.

Taking time to examine your non-verbal signals, understanding and improving them, fitting them for the occasion and the person/people you are communicating with is time well spent. Also learning what to look for in others can help you understand what is being conveyed.

Get the right inner voice

Before meeting someone you need to ensure that your inner voice is correct. If it is saying:

I am wary

I am nervous

I don't really like this person

I don't want to be here

I don't think I am going to understand this person

then how do you think your smile and eye contact will look? Yes, it will reflect what you are thinking.

Try to ensure you have a positive inner voice when meeting people including strangers.

For example:

I am confident

I will find this person interesting

I can be warm and welcoming

I am easy in myself and will enjoy meeting this person.

Greetings and introductions

There are many different ways of greeting people depending on the culture of the country you are visiting. It is therefore best to be aware of these if you are doing business abroad or even taking a holiday.

Here we discuss the general forms of greeting:

- eye contact
- smile
- handshake.

There are others of course and here are some of them and what they mean:

- **the handshake and kiss on one cheek** – formal but also more friendly, you know the other person quite well and usually like them
- **the kiss on two cheeks** often holding onto the other persons shoulders- much more friendly
- **the hug** – intimate and very friendly
- **the kiss on the lips** – very intimate and very friendly

- **the smile but no bodily contact** – we know the person but are not that close to them, or feel rather shy or uncomfortable in touching them

Eye contact

There are cultural differences in how much eye contact it is acceptable to give another person when meeting them and listening to them. In Britain, America and Canada quite a lot of eye contact is given between individuals. In Europe less so although research has shown the Greeks prefer a considerable amount of eye contact, the Swedes less so. Arabs are fairly dependent on maintaining eye contact while the Japanese tend to look downward, aiming at a person's neck rather than directly into their eyes.

When you meet someone, you should aim to hold the eye contact while smiling and shaking hands with them and then break eye contact when the other person looks away, or when you finish shaking hands and change your body posture.

Too much eye contact can make the other person feel uncomfortable. It can be used as a dominant gesture and is an invasion of privacy.

If you give too little eye contact it can suggest boredom, disinterest or maybe shyness. Closing the eyes completely when making conversation is a negative signal.

If the person refuses to give you eye contact then try asking a direct question. Once you get eye contact, no matter how fleeting, connect with it and smile to show encouragement and to build rapport.

When flirting our eye contact tends to rove, giving

quick glances accompanied by smiling and laughing. When more serious flirting is taking place the gaze will linger longer and when intimate will move from the eyes to the mouth and occasionally drop to the neck. To deal with unwanted flirting keep your gaze on the business zone, that of eyes and forehead.

The smile

Your smile should be warm and welcoming. Obviously the better you know someone and like them the warmer your smile. We all know, or have met, people who although smiling their eyes show no warmth or welcome and the gesture is an empty one. False smiles are held in place, the lips stiff and stretched and the eyes stay unsmiling. This is also often an aggressive and sometimes dominant stance and can be used as a gesture to keep people at their distance.

> Smiling is good for you.

Smiling helps to ward off viruses and can alleviate stress as can laughter. If you smile more you will find that your day is brighter and easier, that people will return your smile, that you feel happier, you discover more information, you get greater cooperation from others. It's got be worth it, hasn't it?

The handshake

The handshake is a very powerful body language gesture. You can form an instant impression of someone by the way they shake hands with you and it can also tell you a considerable amount about the person you are dealing with. Until recently the handshake was predominantly a male body language gesture and women, unless they were of a higher social class, did not shake hands. However, times have changed and there are now many more women in business and the workplace and so both men and women use the handshake.

The friendly handshake

When you greet someone you should walk forwards with your arm outstretched, not too stiff but with your elbow tucked into your waist. You should smile and hold the other person's eye contact.

As I mentioned above, since the handshake is not the usual form of greeting for women, many men are not sure if they should shake hands with women. So, in order to eliminate this problem, women should offer their hand first.

Your handshake should be firm and dry. It is not always easy to know if you are giving a good handshake, as people won't tell you. To find out what your handshake is like why not shake hands with someone whose opinion you trust and ask them honestly to tell you. Do you need to firm it up? Is it perhaps too strong and you need to relax it a little?

Take the whole hand and not just the fingertips. Do not pump the hand but shake it and then release it.

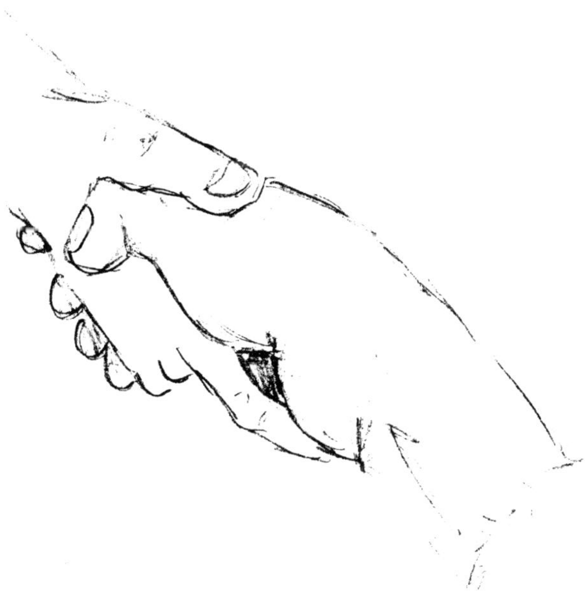

Building rapport through the handshake

Be attuned to the person you are shaking hands with. If they give you a firm handshake try and return the pressure, not so that you get into a wrestling match with them but just slightly. If their handshake is weaker than yours, then relax yours. This is all part of building rapport. You are in fact mirroring their body language – but more about this later.

The dominant person's handshake

Be aware of the length of time you hold onto someone's hand. Too long and this can be viewed as a dominant body language gesture.

I find this particularly irritating and offensive but there is little you can do about it apart from trying to wrest your hand away, which would look silly and be rather pointless. So instead force yourself to keep good steady eye contact with this person, who will also be using dominant eye contact on you – it almost becomes a battle of wills – and keep smiling, not grinning inanely, or aggressively gritting your teeth, but smiling pleasantly.

The dominant person's handshake will be very strong, almost too strong and again, so as to avoid being cast into an inferior role in this relationship, you should return the pressure giving the non-verbal signal that you are no pushover.

The superior person's handshake

This has many of the traits stated above. The superior

(and dominant) person can offer his hand to you from a great distance away; his arm will be outstretched and stiff as he walks towards you, then he will take your hand in his vice-like grip.

He may also do the double clutch handshake, which is sometimes referred to as the Politician's Handshake – watch newsreels to see just how many politicians use this! Here he puts his other hand on top of yours.

Your reaction? Well try putting your hand on top of his like playing 'pat a cake'. By doing this you are effectively saying 'Oh no you're not in charge, I am equally superior and dominant as you 'even if you don't feel you are' – it works.

A variation of this superior body language is where the person shakes your hand but also touches your shoulder.

If this is man-to-man and the other man is known to you then it can be interpreted as a friendly gesture. But if you have just met this man for the first time, or don't know him very well, it can be interpreted as a dominant, superior gesture.

If a man touches a woman's upper arm then it is more of an intimate gesture as is a man touching a woman's back.

Women tend to touch each other more than men and would usually touch the lower arm.

Touching a person's elbow, either man or woman, is a friendly gesture and usually prompts a positive response.

In summary

- the first impression you make can be a lasting impression
- body language includes:

  eye contact and eye movement;

  distance from others e.g. personal space zone;

  posture and stance;

  facial expressions;

  gestures
- non-verbal signals you give out are said to be four and a half times more powerful than your verbal

signals

- your facial expressions at least eight times more powerful as the spoken word
- take time to get to know the various kinds of greetings in different cultures
- before meeting someone ensure that your inner voice is correct
- when you meet someone you should aim to hold the eye contact while smiling and shaking hands
- your smile should be warm and welcoming
- you can form instant impressions of someone by the way they shake hands with you
- your arm should be outstretched, not too stiff but with your elbow tucked into your waist. You should smile and hold the other person's eye contact
- your handshake should be firm and dry
- take the whole hand and not just the fingertips.
- Do not pump the hand but shake it and then release it.

6

Body language in different situations

Entering a crowded room

Nearly everyone at some time feels nervous when entering a crowded room. Even that confident-looking man or woman in the corner probably has butterflies inside them. So how can you alleviate these feelings and make new contacts and friends in this situation?

First make sure you have taken care over your appearance and that you are wearing the appropriate clothes for the occasion. Wear something that makes you feel good, that you know suits you and wear colours that enhance your confidence and not drain it. Also ensure that you are well groomed and for women, wearing make up can considerably enhance your confidence, particularly lipstick.

Many people fear entering a crowded room because they are afraid that everyone will be looking at them. They won't. I promise you that unless you are a famous actor, royal personage, celebrity, or Prime Minister/ President then hardly anyone will even notice you arrive. For show-offs like me I find this most disappointing!

Before you enter that room ensure that your inner voice is correct:

I can handle this

I am confident

I am going to enjoy meeting some new people today

I know you won't trust that inner voice to begin with but remember the body will do what the brain tells it and vice versa.

So put your shoulders back, open your chest, stand tall and ensure that your posture is upright, not too stiff but confident.

One other trick that can help you is to visualize an experience in your life where you felt extremely pleased and proud of yourself, where perhaps you had just achieved something, you'd passed an examination, or your driving test for example. How did you feel then? What was your body language like? Yes, head up, confident, smiling. By evoking this experience you can release the positive thoughts and emotions, your body language will respond accordingly and you will look and become more confident.

SILENCE that awful little negative voice that keeps creeping in saying things like ' I am going to hate this.' 'I can't do this.' 'I wish the ground would swallow me up and I could disappear.' 'I wish I could escape.' Can you see how this kind of inner voice will drag you down, and pull all your body language with it? If you believe you are going to hate it – you **WILL** hate it.

Look for the lone person

Make sure you arrive in plenty of time, neither too early or late. Stand just inside the room and look around you. Now, there are a number of things you can do, all of which I do myself. Look for someone who is standing on his or her own. They may be looking lost; they may be reading the programme or standing with a cup of coffee but they are alone. Move forward and approach them. Don't get too close but keep your personal space distance, smile and give them eye contact. You can then open the conversation by saying

'*Hello, is it all right if I join you?*'

They will, believe me, be overwhelmed with gratitude.

They smile and say, '*Of course.*'

Then you can introduce yourself. Here you may wish to extend your hand, '*I'm Jane Smith.*'

'*Harry Brown.*'

'*Is this your first time here, Harry?*'

or

'*Have you been to one of these events before, Harry?*'

You may have noticed that in my response I have repeated their name. This is an old trick and one that will help you remember their name. It works for me every time.

Don't approach two people standing face to face or a threesome standing in a triangle as their body language is communicating that they do not wish to be interrupted. If you do need to break into a triangle stand just on the edge and wait until there is a change in body language or a natural gap in the conversation.

Join a queue

Another way of making contacts at these types of events is **to join a queue**. There is always a queue: for coffee, for lunch, for signing in, for looking at things on tables etc. It is then very simple to turn to the person behind you or in front of you and start a conversation with something along the lines of:

'I hate these queues, don't you?'

'The food smells nice, doesn't it?'

'I'm really looking forward to my coffee, the journey here was dreadful this morning – did you get held up on the train?'

You can then move into conversation, but more about this in Chapter 8.

Ask questions, for example about their occupation, where they have come from, how they travelled to the venue?

Nod your head to encourage them to talk, keep eye contact relaxed and friendly, smile comfortably and tilt your head to show that you are listening to them. If you are particularly brave lightly touch them on the arm, beneath the elbow, to connect with them.

Do not overstay your welcome or hog them for the entire event but move on and try talking to someone else. As you sit down for example – *'Is this anyone's seat?' 'I'm looking forward to this seminar are you?' 'How far did you have to come today?' 'Have you been to any of these before?'* And you're off.

What if you get stuck with the bore?

Having been brave enough to find someone to talk to, and having opened up the conversation, what happens if you then discover that you are saddled with the seminar nutcase or the complete bore? You have tried your hardest to be nice and to listen but the time has come for you to move on. How do you do this politely?

When you do need to move on you can formalize this by stretching out your hand and saying, *'It's been really nice meeting you/talking to you. I hope you enjoy the show/seminar, have a safe journey home.'* Or you may lightly touch them on the arm, (again below the elbow) smile and say the above without shaking hands, depending on the formality of the gathering.

Sometimes another person will enter your conversation making the group a trio. Hopefully your new contact will introduce you but if they don't introduce yourself offer your hand and say

'Hello I'm xxxx.'

Alternatively you may use this as the time to duck out. Make your apologies, smile and move on.

Personal space

A word about personal space before we move onto interviewing and presentations body language. Personal space is the distance you feel comfortable with when meeting or reacting with another person. It varies from country to country between individuals and genders, and in different situations. For example, the Italians and French have a much closer personal space distance and are more tactile than the British or Germans. The Japanese and Chinese have closer body space zones and in India the personal space zone is practically non-existent.

In Britain the personal space distance is about three feet hence the old saying 'keep them at arm's length', which is approximately three feet. This is why we often feel uncomfortable when someone sits next to us on a bus or train, or at a seminar. It is why we put our bags or briefcases on the seat beside us; we are creating and establishing our own personal space. In crowded places like trains or the Underground in rush hour, or a crowded lift, it is not possible to have the personal space we like around us. In these situations people will often not look at one another but will look at the ceiling or the floor, and/or they will angle their body language away from the other person. Where this is not always possible you will find that we keep our body language movements down to a minimum, keeping very still.

> **Those we like and know we will allow closer to us.**

In the networking situation previously described we need to keep personal space distance between us. If someone we don't know very well gets too close then we tend to back off.

Interviews

Interviews make us nervous so taking time to prepare for an interview will go some way to easing those nerves.

1 Make sure that you are **wearing the right clothes** and that you are **well groomed**, and don't forget those shoes – they need to be clean and well heeled.

2 Get the right inner voice

I can handle this

I am confident

I have prepared well for this interview

I know my strengths and weaknesses and I will give it my best shot.

NOT

I hate interviews

I'm sure I'm going to fail

There are going to be far more qualified/ experienced people than me

I know I won't be able to answer any of their questions

I know I won't get the job

If you hear any of these destructive voices in your head then **SILENCE** them and convert them to a positive inner dialogue (see The Easy Step by Step Guide to *Being Positive and Staying Positive* for more on this).

3 Tell yourself that you are confident, put your shoulders back, open your chest, hold your head up, smile. Shake hands if the interviewer offers his/her hand and remember that your handshake should be dry and firm, taking the whole hand. Give good eye contact.

4 Sit when invited to do so. If you are being interviewed by a panel you may have your chair positioned some distance away from the interviewers. This can be very daunting but maintain that positive inner voice. The panel can see all your body language gestures so ensure you keep your body language open, legs uncrossed, arms and hands resting lightly in front of you on your lap or on the arms of the chair. Keep your body language movements to a minimum but you can angle your body to the speaker/questioner.

5 Sit upright, look and be alert. Sit forward to convey real interest. Keep your eyes on the speaker, moving eye contact to the person who is asking you questions if there is more than one interviewer and then, when you have answered, sweeping your eye contact to the rest of the panel. Remember to smile if you can.

Don't

slouch;

look down at your hands, out of the window, at the ceiling;

fold your arms tightly across your body.

6 In interviews don't threaten the interviewer's personal space by invading it. I saw this happen once when an interviewee lunged across a dividing table at the interviewer who sprang back and completely forgot what she was going to ask. Needless to say the applicant didn't get the job.

We often place a barrier in front of us to mark our personal space. Behind this barrier we feel comfortable and safe. We can also feel superior. Interviewers and bosses do this, which is not always a good interviewing tactic or one for team building, as you cannot get to know the other person with a barrier between you. Doctors used to do this but many no longer do so. However some medical consultants still use this as a way of clearly defining the patient– doctor relationship.

Do not put anything on the interviewer's desk or table without asking permission first and that also goes for the sales interview. The desk or table is their territory and you are invading it if you don't ask their permission.

Giving presentations

Many people are nervous when asked to give a presentation – that is perfectly natural. Your mouth dries up, your hands perspire. The adrenalin rushes in your veins and your heart goes into overdrive. Your contracting stomach robs you of hunger (though afterwards you'll be ravenous), your legs tremble and your voice becomes strained. When we are faced with what we believe is a hostile or difficult situation we experience the **Flight or Fight syndrome**. Your body will prepare itself to either fight the situation or run away from it. Your body can take control but you mustn't allow it too completely. You don't want to eliminate nervousness because you need a certain amount to help you give a better performance – some great actors still suffer terrible stage fright before they perform – so being nervous is natural. It is controlling these nerves that is important.

> American researchers asked 3,000 people what they feared most – 40 per cent gave speaking before a large audience as the affliction they most dreaded.

One of the greatest fears that people have is that all eyes are on them when they stand to present. So instead of thinking about all those people looking at you, you need to reverse it – you must think of yourself as giving out to those people. You must feel (and tell yourself) that it is you who is in control. Also be aware that potentially the audience is more nervous than you are! They want you to be good. They want you to succeed.

Overcoming nervousness

To help overcome nervousness, especially right at the beginning when it is worse, the trick is to divert eyes from you.

Two ways of doing this are:

1 **Put up a visual** and ask people to look at it. That way you can chat quite happily about what is on the chart without people looking at you

2 **Start with a question** to the audience, for example, if your talk is about the increase in violence you could ask, 'How many of you here today are worried about violence in the community?' Hands go up. Then, 'The gentleman in the blue jacket, what particularly worries you?' All eyes are now on him. You can carry on this technique by asking another person in the audience for their opinion.

> Use questions and flip charts to get involvement and draw attention away from you.

When your speech begins stand slowly, keep your hand movements slow and deliberate. Smile. Keep smiling. Let your eyes rove the audience. Don't hurry. Come

out to the front, smile, open your arms in a welcome gesture.

As you start to speak look at everybody in the room. With small groups acknowledge each one with eye contact. With larger groups you'll have spots where you should rest your eyes for a moment and then sweep on to the next. These spots should be dotted around the auditorium. If you don't make eye contact with the back of the hall it is unlikely that your voice will reach the back row either.

Do not be tempted into giving your talk to the only friendly face and ignore the rest. You need to make good steady eye contact with those who look bored and cynical. This takes courage but it works. Someone who appears downright awkward and resistant in an audience can be looking like this because they feel superior to everyone else and/or because the subject is threatening. By making extra eye contact with them they start to feel that you are acknowledging their significance and they feel less threatened because they trust you.

Don't hide behind a lectern or table. It will create a barrier. Equally don't talk to the wall or the flip chart or walk up and down, sway, or keep rising on your toes.

With a large audience the personal space zone is about twelve feet, drawing inwards with smaller audiences.

Watch out for those mannerisms like scratching, rubbing your nose, pulling ears, turning over your loose change in your pockets and fastening and unfastening your jacket.

Always stand rather than sit. Your energy level is different when you stand and you look more powerful. If you are giving a long talk or a training session always stand at the outset to establish authority. When you want to gain confidence and be more like one of the audience then you can sit, i.e. during question and answer sessions.

Don't stand with your hands folded in front of the body in the vicar/fig leaf position or clasped behind your back like a policeman! In the drawing opposite our man has his legs firmly planted apart and a smile on his face with head tilted back, this tends to make him look superior.

Meetings

At some time we all attend meetings, whether this is work related, more of a social nature or a combination

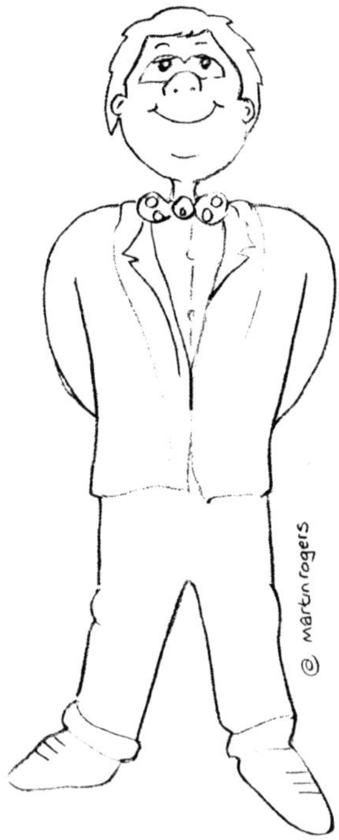

of both. For example you may be on the Parent Teacher Association of a school, or on a charitable fundraising committee. Making an impression at meetings could help you to be heard in that meeting, or you may wish to read others' body language to find out what they really think about your views.

First, where to sit

In meetings if you want recognition always sit within good eye contact of the decision maker (who may not always be the chair). This can often be at the opposite end of the table.

To lessen confrontation sit next to the challenger. It is far more difficult to attack from the side. Avoid sitting directly opposite the person.

If you are a junior or new participant wait to be told where to sit.

If you wish to avoid attention sit in a blind spot for the chair where it is physically difficult for them to see you and wear your most neutral outfit with no special accessories.

Another point about seating which I have often observed is that when both men and women enter a room together, the men will all sit together and the women will sit together. Only if someone is late and there are no empty spaces will the genders divide. In schools and sometimes at work it is a good idea to mix the genders to encourage more cross-gender communication and cooperation. For example, ask all the girls to come into the class first and tell them they must not sit together, then invite the boys to fill up the empty places.

Other ways to enhance your power at meetings

Make sure you find out the objectives of the chairperson if you can. Don't be afraid to contribute your points but if you're out to win or score points only important to you, you may become resented. Never expect to succeed in a meeting on a wing and a prayer. Preparation is essential. Whenever possible, without overdoing it, always try to state your views, or ask an intelligent question.

Resist the temptation to finish other people's sentences or criticize them at a personal level.

Even if you are feeling emotional about an objection

try not to show it. Your detractors will leap on you like a wounded animal if they sense weakness.

Be positive but if you disagree or have reservations say so and have reasons why you disagree to back this up. Show that you can think a thing through logically and laterally.

If you wish to speak hold up your hand and look at the chairperson. Only interrupt if the meeting has more of a casual flavour about it. Women interrupt conversations far more than men, in fact men find this rather irritating. They often wait until someone has finished speaking before having their say, unless the speaker is a waffler or droning on too much and the interrupter is an impatient man.

As chairperson if you wish to shut someone up without verbally telling them then one of the most effective ways is to look away as they are speaking to you, alternatively you can glance at your watch.

You can sit forward and hold your hand up; this is the physical **STOP** sign.

You can also accompany this by saying, 'Hold on', or '*Excuse me*'.

> Never adopt the role of the Disrupter or the Nonentity

The **Disrupter** is the person who arrives late or dashes in and out to take phone calls. This is most irritating and implies superiority; either that or he can't organize or prioritize his time effectively!

The **Nonentity** remains part of the furniture. If you don't or can't participate then you probably won't be invited again. More involvement brings more responsibility but it also means more visibility and hence advancement.

(For more on meetings see The Easy Step by Step Guide to *Fewer, Shorter, Better Meetings*.)

Eye contact

During business meetings you should keep your eye contact on the eyes and forehead of the person who is speaking.

You can use direct eye contact to make a point both in a personal relationship setting and in a business setting, for example when you have a serious point to make or when reprimanding a child.

Do look interested during the meeting, lean your body forward, give good eye contact to the speaker and the chair, make occasional notes.

Don't look bored, doodle, sigh, sniff and shift about

unless you really want to give the wrong impression and not be asked back!

In summary

- before you enter a crowded room, or attend an interview, get the right positive inner voice
- put your shoulders back, stand tall and adopt a confident posture
- stand just inside the room and look for someone who is standing on his or her own
- move forward and approach them, don't get too close and ask if you can join them
- don't approach two people standing together, or a triangle of people
- join a queue and talk to the person behind or in front of you
- do not overstay your welcome, move on
- in interviews sit forward to convey interest, keep your eyes on the speaker, keep your body language open
- when giving a presentation think of yourself as giving out, use open gestures, sweep the room with your eye contact, always stand rather than sit as it helps your energy level
- in meetings sit within good eye contact of the chairperson to be noticed
- to lessen confrontation sit next to the challenger

7

Body language – posture, gestures and stance

When reading body language you need to look at the whole person and the complete picture. Just because someone has his arms crossed it does not necessarily mean he is hostile. If his arms and legs are crossed and he is perhaps scowling or keeping his distance by sitting back in his seat then the complete picture tells you this person is aggressive or hostile and is not going to cooperate.

I recall a course I was running. A woman was sitting at the table with her head in her hands. Did she have a headache, or a hangover perhaps? Or was she hostile? From her body language and the situation I deemed that she was on the course under sufferance and that by withdrawing her eye contact, and her complete facial expressions, she was saying 'I don't want any part in this'; 'I am not going to cooperate'.

So I started by asking her a question, which meant that she had to look up and give me eye contact. I could then begin to engage with her. After several more exchanges, and as the course progressed, she confessed that she hadn't wanted to come on the course but that she was now enjoying it. A victory indeed!

Beware mannerisms

We all form certain mannerisms like pulling the eyebrow, rubbing the nose etc. We need to be aware of these because they may be giving out the wrong signals. The best way to know if you are doing this is to watch a video recording of yourself, or get a friend to tell you each time you make a nervous mannerism.

Some years ago I was working with a young lady who always put her hand over her mouth when she spoke. This gave out the impression that she was lying or was uncertain of herself. I asked her why she did this and she told me that when she was younger she suffered from terrible acne, which caused her considerable distress and embarrassment so she had got into the habit of covering her face when she spoke so people couldn't see her skin. The habit had stuck long after her skin had cleared.

Here are some further body language signals that you might like to be aware of.

Dominant or aggressive body language

Sitting down with the hands and arms clasped behind the head

This is a superior gesture or exhibits extreme confidence sometimes bordering on arrogance. It can also be accompanied by the chin held high.

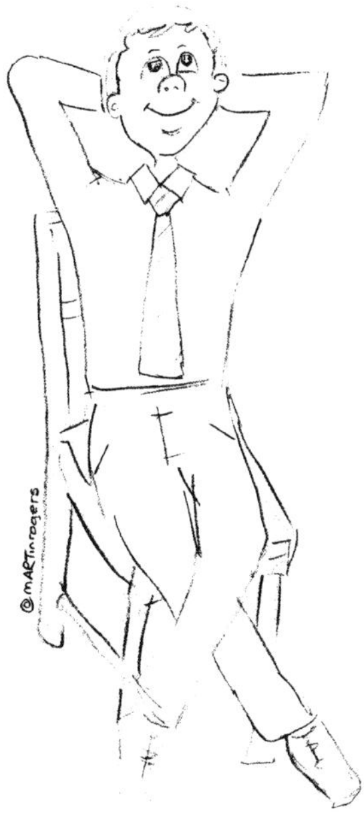

Leg lock – when one ankle is crossed over the knee of the other.

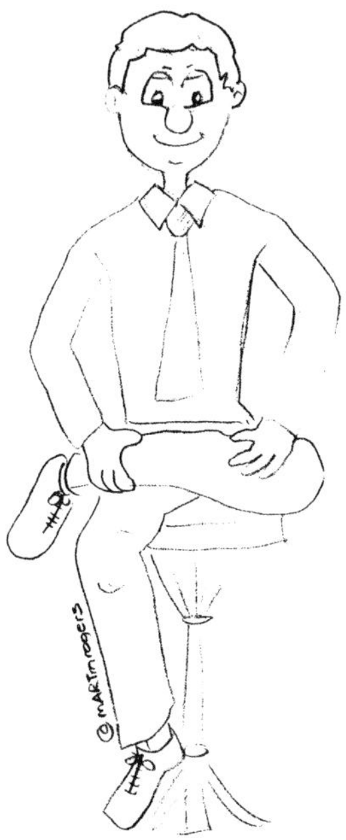

This denotes a dominant and competitive personality. The higher the leg is crossed over the more dominant and competitive. If the person is also holding his leg this means he is stubborn and unmoving, he's made his mind up.

If the thumbs are on display in an upward position this shows that they are in charge! This is often a familiar stance of a barrister in a courtroom. Some speakers also adopt this posture, which can be rather intimidating towards the audience. In the drawing here our lady has both her thumbs on display in an upward position and has also crossed her arms, she is definitely in charge and has made up her mind. She will be impossible to convince.

Another variation of this is when the thumbs protrude from the pockets, which displays dominance.

Thumbs wrapped round belt

If a man is standing with his legs firmly planted apart, thumbs in belt pose, with fingers pointing down towards crotch area this is an aggressive posture when adopted facing another man.

If, however, a man adopts this posture towards a woman then it can be interpreted as a sexual gesture. In recent years some women have also adopted this posture, in this instance it exhibits an attitude of dominance and sexual control over men.

Hands on hips

This is an aggressive and threatening gesture when used by a man or when used by a woman to another woman. If a woman adopts this posture towards a man then it can be interpreted as a sexual stance.

Nervous body language

One hand gripping the other behind the back is an attempt at confidence but there is frustration, lack of self-control and the person is trying hard to seem relaxed – look for how hard the hand is gripping the wrist. If the hands are held quite high behind the back this often indicates timidity. The hand moved even further up the arm indicates tension and nervousness.

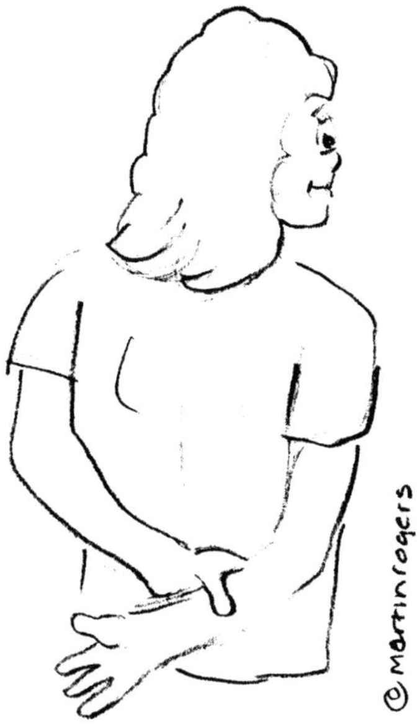

Fingers in the mouth can also show people under pressure.

Touching the face or stroking the back of the neck can signal embarrassment and rubbing, stroking or touching the nose means the person is not sure and possibly has negative thoughts; if poor or no eye contact accompanies this then he could be lying.

Touching the ear may indicate that the person doesn't like what he/she is hearing. Watch for this in meetings and sales situations and examine what it is you have just said to get this response.

Touching the eyes could indicate that the person doesn't like what he or she is seeing. Watch for a shifting in body language along with this and consider the situation and the dialogue.

Foot lock – this tends to be a woman-only gesture where one foot is wrapped round the other leg. It is construed as a defensive attitude.

Assertive body language

Assertive body language is used when the person is confident and has good self-esteem. The posture is upright but not stiff, head up but not tilted too far back. The body language is generally open and relaxed with good eye contact and a natural smile.

Hand resting lightly on cheek – this is analysing and listening

Body pointing – the feet will point towards the person in the group that they are most interested in.

Pupils – When someone is interested in someone else his or her pupils will enlarge or more correctly dilate.

Steepling – Linking your hands together as though to form a steeple prevents you making nervous mannerisms. If you have a table in front of you, with your hands linked you are staking out your territory. This gesture also suggests confidence and self-possession.

Stillness suggests ease and comfort in a situation, especially the ability to keep the hands and feet still and relaxed.

When it comes to reading and understanding body language girls' and hence women's eye contact is better than boys. Girls and therefore women use more body language than men and are able to read it better.

In summary

- be attuned to body language. Look for the whole picture
- beware of mannerisms and check that you are not giving out the wrong body language signals.

8
Opening and structuring conversations

So far then we have got our inner voice right in that it is telling us we are confident and calm, that we are in control and can handle things. We have taken care of our appearance, making sure we are wearing the right clothes that suit us with colours that enhance us and we are well groomed. We have picked up some tips on body language and we know how to evoke positive body language by recalling to mind a positive past experience, by putting our shoulders back and standing tall and we have practised our eye contact and handshake. We now need to know how to open and structure conversations.

We have already looked at how to open some conversations when we examined how to enter a crowded room and strike up a conversation with a stranger; we are now going to build on this.

Open questions

In order to open conversations we need to use **open questions.** These start with the following words:

What

Where

When

How

Why

Who

By beginning your conversations with these words you will get even the most reluctant of conversationalists to open up.

You may think that you already use open questions but believe me many people don't and instead they resort to asking **closed questions**, which of course are designed to close the conversation down. Closed questions usually elicit a single word response, yes or no.

Closed questions

Closed questions begin with:

Is

Are

Should

Could

Shall

Will

Would

Do/Did

For example:

'Do you come here often?' **(closed)**

Answer: *'No.'*

Or

'How often do you come here?' **(open)**

'Oh, several times a month.'

'What do you think of it?' **(open)**

'It's all right I suppose, it could be better though.'

'Oh how?' **(open)**

'Well I think ...' he's off ...

Whereas if we ask closed questions, see how much more difficult this would be:

'Do you come here often?' **(closed)**

'Yes.'

'How many times do you come?' **(open)**

'Once or twice a month.'

'Is it any good?' **(closed)**

'It's all right?'

'Oh.'

I am struggling to make conversation. It is much more stilted and if you start by asking a closed question you end up having to ask more questions, two in the last example to my one in the first example. This makes conversation particularly difficult if the person you are with is not a natural communicator.

Listen to any child and count the number of open questions they ask: *'Why do I have to go to bed now Mummy?' 'Why can't I have any sweets?' 'What time is it?' 'How far is it now?' 'What's that man doing?'* and so on because they are hungry for knowledge and this is how they find out. But as we get older we stop becoming so curious, sometimes we are told not to ask so many questions, not to pry, so we shut up which is a shame.

> **In order to improve your communication and become a good conversationalist you need to relearn the lost art of asking open questions.**

And yes, you do have to learn it and practice it because you have probably fallen into bad habits by asking closed questions.

If we return to our crowded room scenario you can see how important it is to ask open questions to break the ice and get the conversation going.

'How far have you come today?'

'What do you do for a living?'

'How many times do you come to these events?'

I am not saying that you never ask closed questions – of course you do – but try rephrasing these into open ones and see if this can make it easier for you to get the other person talking and help you over those difficult first moments.

Gender differences

A word here about gender differences. Men and women open conversations with different topics and it might be helpful for you to know this when striking up a conversation with a member of the opposite sex.

How men break the ice

When two men meet they will often try to find common ground through three main areas: sport (usually football), cars and sometimes women. But if they are meeting in a formal or professional setting then they will talk about their jobs. But before they even get onto any of these three (or four topics) they will discuss their journey to the meeting, seminar, party, reunion or function in great and almost nauseating detail! This is how the conversation might go between two men talking at a function in London after the greeting has taken place:

'So where have you come from today?'

'From Portsmouth on the South Coast, do you know it?'

'Yes, had an uncle who lived there once that's about seventy miles away isn't it?'

'Yes. What about you?'

'Manchester.'

'How long did it take you to get here?'

'Two hours.'

'That's not bad. Which way did you come?'

Here the other man gives a detailed description naming every road by its proper reference i.e. M3 etc. *'Got held up at junction 11 though but I managed to bypass that using the A123.'*

'I know that road, it's a good little route that.'

'What about you?'

'Simple, A3M, A3 straight into London, left before the rush hour so did it in an hour and a half, would have done it quicker if it wasn't for the roadworks on the bypass.'

'That's good going ...'

And so on. It becomes a kind of competition, each man showing off his navigation prowess and his driving skills. And if you don't believe me just listen next time you are at a function! Every woman should already know that men do not like being criticized over their driving, they never get lost and even if they do, they did it on purpose just to try out a different route!

How women start conversations

When two women meet they will search for common ground through their social background: family, partner, hobbies, friends, where they live etc. Men call this gossiping but it isn't, not to women. It is why when a man and woman return home after the function and the woman starts telling her partner all about that nice woman she met from number twenty-two she can tell him her life history. The man is often amazed, flabbergasted even, saying something like *'How on earth did you manage to find all that out?' 'Simple,'* she says, *'I just asked her'*.

You will also find that women cross-talk a lot more than men, each interrupting the other and interjecting into the conversation whereas men will take it in turns to talk.

If a woman enters an all male meeting she will often find that the men are discussing last night's football game, or some other sporting event, or they are talking about cars and their performance. So let's say she's an expert on football and cars, and decides to interject. Instead of finding that she is welcomed into the conversation with her contribution, she will draw some blank expressions from the men around the table. After looking at her the men will continue talking among themselves and the woman will feel hurt or angry, believing that she has been snubbed. She hasn't, not deliberately, it's just that men don't expect a woman to talk 'their' language.

This does not always apply to a man breaking into a woman's conversation with chatter about the kids, the partner, or the house because some men have the female style of communication and they find it very easy to talk to women and indeed get on very well with them. Women feel very comfortable around these men and like talking to them. My husband is one of these and consequently is very popular with the ladies! Any man reading this book who has a limited conversation centred around sport and cars should take a tip from me, develop your conversational skills by asking women about their family, themselves, their hobbies, using friendly open questions and I can guarantee you that your chatting up technique and your relationships will greatly improve.

OK, so let's move on. We start with open questions and we seek every opportunity to improve these. At every party or social function you attend, practise your questioning techniques. I usually aim to find at least one person I do not know and I set myself a target to find out everything I possibly can about that person before I move on or leave. They might never find out anything about me because once I have got them talking they are very happy to chatter on about themselves. Try it yourself. Don't stick with the familiar faces and friends, move out of your comfort zone and find someone new to talk to: even if you never see them again you have sharpened up your approach and your questioning technique.

Other ways of opening conversations include paying the other person a compliment. I use this quite a lot myself. I enjoy paying people compliments and enjoy the pleasure it gives others. I have even been known to strike up conversations with complete strangers in the Ladies toilet by saying; 'I love your suit/coat. It looks really nice on you, where did you get it?' (Notice I have ended by asking an open question).

The weather is of course (in Britain at least) an endless topic of conversation as is the traffic, parking or the promptness of the trains.

For example, 'The traffic was horrendous this morning, and then I couldn't park. Where did you park?'

In order to expand your conversation skills, expand your reading. Keep abreast of current events, know what is happening in your area, your country. Cultivate a wide range of interests. Try and find some common ground but don't go on and on about your own views or experiences, just drop them in and then ask a question to get the other person talking. Take an interest in them, don't become a bore.

Building conversations

Now we need to look at building conversations. Once you have started people talking you need to probe a little bit more with those open questions digging deeper to keep them going.

Let's take an example

'Where did you go on holiday this year?' **(open)**

'New Zealand.'

'Really, how interesting. It's a place I've always wanted to go but not had the chance yet; what was it like?' **(I have disclosed my own feelings without going on about them and then asked an**

open, probing question to get the other person talking again)

'Oh, it's fantastic. It's such a beautiful place, so much to do and see and the people are great.'

'Whereabouts did you go?' **(open)**

'Oh all over, both Islands, we toured most of the time and then we stayed with my brother in Auckland.'

'Oh you've got a brother there, aren't you lucky? I don't know anyone living there but I've read so much about it. How long has your brother lived there?' **(I have added in a little more information about me but followed it up with an open probing question)**

'Twelve years now, this was the first time I'd seen him since he emigrated there.'

'That must have been great. What made him emigrate?' **(empathising with his feelings/experience and following it up with an open probing question)**

With this type of questioning I could have this person telling me his life history in no time at all. I have used open questions and I have probed a bit deeper. I have also employed a couple of other techniques; I have added in some of my own thoughts and feelings i.e. *'It's a place I've always wanted to go but not had the chance to yet; what was it like?'* and I have empathized with his experience i.e. *'That must have been great.'* I have also repeated one of his statements in a reflective way, *'Oh, you've got a brother there.'*

So in the above example I have added interest to the conversation by being:

- **reflective:** repeating statements in a reflective way
- **empathic**: identifying with the emotions around

that person's experience

- **supportive**: being encouraging and reassuring. But we can also add the following into conversations:
- **exploratory:** *'What happened after that?'*
- **clarifying:** *'So what you're saying is …'*

  'Do you mean that?'

  'I'm not sure I understand …'
- **Interpreting**

  'Are you perhaps saying …'

Let's pick up on our New Zealand example at the last question and see where we go with this conversation.

'What made him emigrate?' **(open probing)**

'He got made redundant from his company in the UK and thought he'd try New Zealand, he'd always wanted to go there.'

'Really why is that?' **(open probing)**

'Just a boyhood dream really.'

'So if he hadn't been made redundant he might never have lived his dream?' **(Interpreting)**

'Absolutely – I'm thinking of moving there too.'

'Would you be able to get a job there?' **(closed)**

'Oh yes, I'm a system analyst and I've already put out feelers.'

'That's very enterprising of you. So if you get the offer of a job you'll go?' **(Clarifying)**

'Yes, if I can persuade my wife.'

'Why, doesn't she want to go?' **(open)**

'Well it's hard to leave all your friends and family and start somewhere new.'

'Yes, it is, very hard. I had to do that when I moved from the UK to live in America for five years.' **(Self-disclosing)**

Can you count in the above example how many closed questions I've asked? Yes, one.

So we have successfully built a conversation. I know this is a lot to think about and that we don't generally go around deconstructing conversations to understand them but by doing this we can see the elements that are required to make for more confident conversations.

Women generally find making conversations easier than men because girls speak earlier than boys. This is because the language part of their brain is developed earlier. This in turn is improved further by the way in which girls play; they build stories around their dolls and their toys enacting out conversations and different scenarios. Boys are much more object-based, preferring to play with cars, soldiers, guns, monsters, spacemen etc. and tend to build a series of noises around their toys rather than having conversations and enacting stories.

In addition, we tend to speak louder to boys and use more commands, *'Jim, put that away, now!'* rather than explaining things to them, which we do with girls. Boys are *told* what to do whereas girls are usually *asked, 'Jane, could you please put that away?'*

In order to improve a boy's skill in communicating we need to add more language by asking him to explain things and by giving him more explanation. We need to encourage boys to express their feelings, which in turn will help them to express themselves more openly when they grow into adulthood.

Then, of course, there is the other half of this equation – in order for communication to be successful we also have to listen; more about that in Chapter 11. But before we move on to improving our listening skills we need to explore what we say and how we speak in more detail to add more confidence to our communications.

In summary

- in order to open conversations you need to ask open questions
- closed questions usually elicit a single word response, often a yes or no
- when two men meet they try to find common ground through talking about sport, cars, work or women
- when two women meet they try to find common ground through talking about their families, partners, and backgrounds
- women cross-talk more than men, interrupting each other
- to expand your conversation skills expand your reading
- experiment with the types of questions you ask,
  be reflective;
  be empathic;
  be supportive;

clarify what you have heard;

interpret and check back with the speaker that you have understood what they are saying.

9

How we speak

Cast your mind back to those first impressions.

55 per cent is based on what we see (appearance and body language)

38 per cent on how we speak

7 per cent on the actual words we are speaking

We have examined the 55 per cent 'what we see' and to some extent the 7 per cent when we looked at building our conversations but there is more to it than this, and a great deal more to how we speak, plus some fundamental differences between what *he* says and what *she* says.

In the previous chapter we looked at questioning techniques to help us build conversations. We also need to understand the structure of how we speak.

The structure of speech

This can be described in three stages.

- **descriptive**
- **reflective**
- **speculative**

For example we might say:

'Nice day' **(Descriptive)**

'Better than yesterday' **(Reflective)**

'I wonder if it will last?' **(Speculative)**

Now there are some differences between the way men and women use this structure.

When men talk they often miss out the reflective stage i.e. the 'better than yesterday' part. So their conversation might go something like this:

'Nice day, hope it lasts.'

Whereas when women speak they often miss out the speculative phase i.e. the *'I wonder if it will last?'* part. So their conversation might go something like this:

'Nice day, isn't it? Better than yesterday.'

This has implications for communication in the workplace and of course in personal relationships.

An example.

In a meeting when there is a problem to be solved, or some procedure or matter is up for discussion, men will often launch straight into the solution, or they might state the problem and then launch into the solution, missing out the reflective part of the conversation. For example:

'As I see it we've got a problem meeting these delivery dates so what we'll do is alter the production schedule.'

Whereas a woman might say *'As I see it we have a problem meeting these delivery dates because we've overstretched ourselves taking on the South African order.'*

She misses out the speculative stage, i.e. the solution.

Or:

He says, *'Staff motivation is a real problem in this office, what we'll do is take everyone out on a team-building day.'*

She says, *'Staff motivation is a real problem in this office, that's because we can never get to talk things through with management and we feel that we really don't matter at all.'*

When a man hears this he is thinking *'I know there's a problem with staff motivation: why doesn't she suggest a solution?'* Or *'I know we've got a problem with delivery dates but what's her solution?'* He will then try and solve the problem by saying, *'OK, if the staff feel like that why don't we all get together for a team-building day!'*

But she says, *'No, that's not the issue.'*

'Well what is?' he replies irritably.

*'We need to discuss **why** we have poor motivation.'*

*'I don't want discussions I want to know **how** we can solve it,'* he snaps.

> Men ask how first – women ask why.

Sometimes men miss out the descriptive stage in their speech altogether and go straight to the speculative i.e. the solutions.

For example he comes into the meeting and says, *'Right, what we're going to do is bring forward production.'* Or *'OK, I've arranged for us all to go on a team building day.'*

The women are thinking – **why?** In addition they feel disorientated because he hasn't followed the stages of speech, which they prefer.

Understanding these differences can help us to improve our communication skills both at work and in our personal lives.

Because women like to go through the stages of speech men should give them more time to explain themselves and then should prompt for the solution i.e. the speculative. Women need to train themselves to think through to a solution or solutions to the problem and then be confident enough to offer them.

Now let's add another layer to this by applying it to the four part statement.

The four-part statement

This is an excellent tool to help you deal with difficult situations and people. It also takes into consideration the gender differences in communication.

The four-part statement:

When you do/say that	**(Descriptive)**
I feel	**(Reflective)**

Because

In future can you/I'd prefer (Speculative)

An example

Your teenage daughter refuses to clean and tidy her bedroom.

He says, *'Go and tidy your room.'* **(Speculative)**

Daughter ignores him.

He says, *'Your room is a pigsty, go and tidy it.'* **(Descriptive and Speculative).**

Daughter still ignores him or moans about him to her mother.

So let's try this again.

He says, *'Your room is so untidy,* ***why*** *don't you tidy and clean it regularly?'*

Daughter says, *'Because I don't feel like it. I'm the one living in it and I think it's OK.'*

He says, *'Yes, I agree, but there are other people living in this house and I feel quite hurt when you don't keep it clean. To save me nagging you all the time,* ***why*** *don't we agree a timetable that suits us both,* ***what*** *do you think would be best?'* **(open question)**

Depending on your teenager you'll either get a grunt, an amazed stare as if you'd gone mad, or a flounce out of the room but you **might** just get a grudging, *'OK then I'll do it once a fortnight.'*

There is another solution of course, simply close the door on the mess, grit your teeth and only do something about it when strange smells start to emit from the room!

It may not be the best example in the world but it worked for a friend of mine.

If we return to Carol and the problems she is having with her mother-in-law who constantly criticizes her, this framework could help her to tackle this. Before we use it though remember we need to think about *why* her mother-in-law is behaving like she is; we looked at this in Chapter 2. We also need to get the right positive inner voice, which we examined in Chapter 3.

So the next time mother-in-law says something which Carol finds hurtful Carol needs to tackle it and say:

'When you say things like that to me, Mary, I feel very hurt and upset because I believe I do a good job raising my children and your grandchildren, in future I'd rather you didn't say such things.'

Mother-in-law might get in a huff or go on the defensive, *'I don't know what you mean; you always take things so personally. That's your trouble, you're too sensitive.'*

Can you see what's happened here? Mother-in-law has shifted the blame back onto Carol, it's Carol's fault! And she's heaped another criticism on to Carol by telling her she is **too sensitive**. She's used this as a put down. Rather than get embroiled in a row that Carol will never win, her best tactic here is to repeat her speculative statement in a quiet, controlled manner. *'I do a good job raising my children and I'd prefer you to keep such remarks to yourself.'*

Mother-in-law may still be huffy but Carol, having said her piece, should move the conversation on, or walk away, giving mother-in-law time to think over her words.

Carol has answered the put down by restating her belief that she is good at raising her children and that she wishes her mother-in-law not to make such hurtful remarks in the future. Her mother-in-law will now think twice before criticizing.

But what if she doesn't? She may try it on again. And if she does what should Carol do? Again keeping a calm, quietly controlled voice (even if her knees are knocking and her heart is pounding) Carol should say, *'We spoke about this before, Mary, I'd prefer it if you didn't make such remarks.'* Carol shouldn't try and justify herself again by giving reasons because she has already done this. If she does try and explain again she is likely to be drawn into further debate or argument, which is probably what her mother-in-law wants or expects.

You may also have noticed that I have used the mother-in-law's name in the conversation. This is another good tactic. It sounds assertive and helps you to connect with the other person.

Now what if mother-in-law tells tales out of school to her son, elaborating Carol's words and using emotional blackmail by pretending to be upset? Carol's husband, Michael, says he'll talk to Carol.

He says, *'Mum's upset why don't you just try and make an effort to get on with her?'* (Here he has used **Descriptive** and **Speculative** statements).

Carol probably feels like spitting blood at this or lashing out at her husband. If she does, and it ends up in a row, who has won? Yes, mother-in-law. Although Carol may be furious with her husband for taking his mother's part and resentful that she has to make all the effort here, she could say,

'Michael, your mother is upset because I told her that when she criticizes me I find it very hurtful and that I would prefer it if she didn't make such remarks. I realize she is alone and perhaps frightened but that doesn't mean she can be hurtful. I will make an effort to understand her if she will make an effort to understand me. Perhaps then we might all get along better.'

And what about Michael? What should he have said to his mother instead of telling her he'll speak to Carol?

Perhaps he should have said, calmly and assertively, *'Mum, I have every confidence in Carol, she looks after the children very well, we are both happy with the way things are.'*

This is not the easiest of situations and until you know why mother-in-law is behaving the way she is, it is difficult to resolve. But until you pluck up the courage to deal with it, it will always be this way. You may like to refer to another technique I use to handle this kind of aggressive and difficult situation in Chapter 13.

Before it gets to this stage though it might be an idea for Carol to try and build rapport with her mother-in-law at different times. Choosing an opportunity when they are alone together she could say, *'Losing your husband so young must have been a terrible experience for you, Mary?'* **(Empathic – identifying with her emotions around the experience)**

'How did you cope with it?' **(Open probing)** *'I don't know what I would do in that situation.'*

'No, I don't suppose you would know', says mother-in-law.

Now Carol can choose to get upset or annoyed over yet another put down or she could silently count to five before answering, ten even if her blood is still boiling, and then say, *'Yes, it's so hard to tell how each of us would react in such circumstances because we are all different.'* Then she should smile and change the subject, telling herself that she can handle this and keep calm.

By treating this put down calmly as a genuine remark, rather than getting emotional and thinking how it hurts her, Carol can handle it confidently.

In summary

- the structure of how we speak is:

  descriptive;

  reflective;

  speculative
- men often miss out the reflective stage and sometimes the descriptive stage going straight to the speculative or the solution
- women often miss out the speculative stage
- he says 'How are we going to solve the problem?'
- she says, 'Why have we got the problem?'
- women follow steps in conversation much more methodically than men
- practice the four-part statement to handle difficult situations and people

  When you say/do;

  I feel;

  Because;

  I'd rather/prefer/would like.

(For more on building assertiveness see the Easy Step by Step Guide, *Being Positive and Staying Positive*)

10
Watch your language

In order to communicate more confidently we need to watch our language, and I don't mean avoiding abusive words, I mean *how* you speak. If you pepper your speech with qualifying statements you will weaken the power of what you are saying. For example:

'Do you know what I mean?'

'You know?'

'Can you understand what I'm saying?'

If you end each sentence with an inflection – a question mark in your voice – you are effectively checking that others approve before continuing to talk. You will sound hesitant. Women tend to do this far more than men.

In addition, check if you use too many fillers like:

er

um

actually

basically
in fact

A good way to see if you are guilty of this is to record yourself, listen to how many fillers, inflections and qualifying statements you use in your voice. Or ask a colleague to count up how many times you use these in the course of an ordinary conversation. We all pick up bad habits and can then find them difficult to shed.

Don't be too apologetic

When you need to state something keep it brief and to the point: don't go all around the houses to make your point or over-apologize. For example try saying, *'I'd like to get started this week'*, or *'Would you like to come over for a coffee?'* Not, *'I wonder if you'd mind terribly if we er sort of started this next week?'* Or *'I was wondering if you've got nothing else to do, that is if you're not too busy, if you'd er like to come over for a coffee?'*

Be careful too of over justifying yourself. For example, *'I wouldn't normally mention this but I'm without the car tomorrow, my husband's had to take it to work because he's got to go to London on business and the trains are on strike and I was wondering if you'd mind giving me a lift into work?'*

Instead simply say, *'Could you give me a lift into work tomorrow Alan as I'm without the car?'*

> If you need to apologize don't do it profusely, simply say, 'I'm sorry'. Or if you wish to sound more assertive, then 'I apologize'.

Practise using 'I' statements, which are assertive, for example:

I feel

I think

my idea is

I prefer

I feel

as I see it

my view is

And be careful of using phrases that put you down, for example:

'I'm hopeless at this.'

'You know me, I seem to be useless at ...'

'I can't seem to ...'

People will believe it and so will you because your brain is telling you that you can't do something so you won't be able to!

Powerful and persuasive words are often those with many vowels in them, for example **need** and **please.**

'We **need** to do something' implies urgency and people respond to this rather than 'We **could** do something', which implies a question mark in its structure. We **must** do something sounds more like a command possibly prompting the response 'Do I have to?' or 'Must I?' While, 'You must appreciate' can prompt the response,'Why must I?'

Tone, pitch and pace

How we sound when we speak does influence others and I am not just talking about accents (although those do give out an impression) but rather the tone of your voice, its clarity, its passion and enthusiasm, its variances.

Think about how you talk to someone who is ill – gently and with compassion and understanding. Now think about how you greet an old friend across the street, or prevent a child from running out into the traffic. How do you sound when you scold someone or are short-tempered?

If you talk in a monotone you will sound dull and uninteresting; you will also lack credibility. The more credible you are the more persuasive you will be. No one is going to do anything if you ask them in a boring, quiet monotone!

So try varying the pitch and pace of your voice. Try enthusing it with some passion. A good way of practising this is to read aloud to young children because then you have to put in all the different voices or they very quickly get bored.

If you talk in a high pitched voice (mainly women) so that you sound like a little girl, you will also be less credible. Try slowing your voice down, don't talk so quickly, take a few more breaths in between talking and lower your voice.

As a general rule speak with clarity, talk in a strong, steady voice neither shouting nor mumbling. If talking to a group of people then let your eye contact reach the person the furthest distance from you to ensure that you project it.

To build rapport with someone match the pace and tone of their voice. I don't mean mimic them but if they speak softly and slowly then lower your voice and slow it down. If the other person speaks quickly, try and quicken up.

No matter what your message, present it in terms that are of interest to others. Think of who you are communicating with and then decide how you should pitch your voice and what sort of words to use. We are all aware of the person/people who talk jargon either to confuse us or to make us feel small, so make sure you don't fall into this trap and if you are on the receiving end of this then don't apologize, to them, for example: *'I'm sorry, I don't understand you'*. It is their fault they are not explaining to you correctly so simply say, *'What do you mean?'* pleasantly and not aggressively.

Believe you are worth listening to and convey that belief to others. The more passionate you are about your subject the more powerful your communication but beware you don't get too carried away and forget your listener, you could be too enthusiastic and alienate them. Which brings us to our next chapter, listening.

In summary

- if you pepper your language with qualifying statements you will weaken the power of your speech
- beware of using too many fillers like um, er, basically
- record your voice to see how it sounds and think of ways of improving it
- don't be too apologetic, use assertive statements like 'I' statements
- if your voice is too high pitched, slow down and

lower your voice

- if you talk in a monotone learn to vary your pitch and pace, practice by reading aloud to young children
- to build rapport with someone match the pace and tone of their voice
- believe you are worth listening to and convey that belief to others

11
Listening

Listening, really listening, is the hardest thing to do and the highest form of courtesy!

Listening is an essential part of being a good communicator but it is a skill that is perilously close to becoming extinct. As more and more of our communication becomes visual and text driven, i.e. Internet, text and computers we are forgetting how to listen. Listening involves both:

the ability to **understand what is being said**,

and the ability to **organize and analyze** the messages in order to retain them for subsequent use.

There are two types of listening:

1 casual listening

2 critical listening

Casual listening

Casual listening is what we tend to do most of the time. We are only half listening, we retain bits of the conversation, we discard other parts of it. As a result you often get the following scenario between two people:

'Don't forget we're going out tonight.'

'Are we? You didn't mention it.'

'Yes, I did, I told you two days ago. You weren't listening.'

We often switch off, particularly when we are listening to someone we know well.

Critical listening

Critical listening requires concentration and stamina. Here you are making a real effort to understand the other person's point of view. You are listening to them, retaining what they say, storing it away and then retrieving some of it later when you need it. These skills are essential in a sales situation and rather important too in an interview. If you have listened, and I mean really listened, it is highly likely that you will come away with a headache. You have exercised your mental powers to extremes! In both the above situations you are not only trying to concentrate on what the other person is saying but you are also reading their body language, thinking about your own body language and formulating your response to their questions, plus thinking of your own questions to ask. Is it no wonder you end up with a headache?

What stops us listening?

There are many things that prevent us from listening, not least of which is laziness. We simply can't be bothered. Or maybe we've never been trained to listen. Our upbringing is such that no one has listened to us so why should we listen to them? No one has taught us how to listen.

The first thing we need to do is to open our minds and have the desire to learn this skill – after all it is good manners to listen. But what prevents us?

- **different perspectives:** we see things differently to the person talking and we disagree with them
- **strong emotions:** we have very strong feelings on the subject which prevents us from listening; we may also have prejudices
- **physical tiredness or discomfort:** we may be tired or hungry; we may be hot or cold; we may be under stress and feel anxious or unwell
- **desire to talk:** we love to talk most of the time, to be the centre of attention; we love the sound of our own voice and think that only our opinions really count
- **distractions and mind wandering:** we may be distracted because of a noise; or we may be thinking ahead of all the things that need to be done; we may be worried about someone or something
- **reactions to the speaker:** we may dislike the person who is talking to us; we may find them boring or opinionated

So how can we improve our listening skills?

Here are some tips to help you:

- start listening with the first word and then listen intently
- stop what you are doing and listen – don't be tempted to do two things at once
- turn off all negative thoughts you have about the speaker
- think at the speed they're talking, don't jump ahead
- do not interrupt
- find an area of interest
- judge the content and not the delivery
- suspend your judgement and keep an open mind
- actively listen for ideas
- resist distractions if you possibly can
- make listening noises, particularly if you are on the telephone, for example 'uh, uh, yes', and if face-to-face ensure that your body language looks as if it is listening, give good eye contact.

Exercises for improving your listening skills

1 Take five minutes a day to sit quietly somewhere, close your eyes and listen to all the sounds around you. Become conscious of them. How many different sounds can you hear? In addition to improving your listening skills this can also be relaxing.

2 When you are having a conversation with another person, receive what he or she has said before rushing in to make your contribution. If you feel you want to interrupt, think about pausing and breathing before you start to talk. A pause before you speak can also add significance.

3 Listen to the radio as much as possible - talk programmes, not music. What information did you receive? Can you summarize it?

In summary

- listening is an essential part of being a good communicator
- listening involves:

  the ability to understand what is being said;

  the ability to organize and analyze the messages in order to retain them for subsequent use.
- there are two types of listening:

  casual listening;

  critical listening
- casual listening is what we tend to do most of the time; we are only half listening
- critical listening requires concentration and stamina
- there are many things that prevent us from listening which include:

  mental laziness;

  different perspectives;

  strong emotions;

physical tiredness or discomfort;
desire to talk;
distractions and mind wandering;
reactions to the speaker

- to improve our listening skills we need to:
  start listening with the first word and then listen intently;
  stop what you are doing and listen;
  turn off all negative thoughts you have about the speaker;
  think at the speed they're talking;
  do not interrupt;
  find an area of interest;
  judge the content and not the delivery;
  suspend judgement;
  actively listen for ideas;
  resist distractions;
  make listening noises.

12

Getting on someone's wavelength

The more you have in common with someone the easier it is to get along with them.

We are more easily influenced by those we like hence the saying, 'people buy people', as any salesperson worth his salt should know. If we like someone we are more inclined to buy from them and to cooperate with them.

Conflict usually results from differences or perceived differences between people. So enhancing this likeability factor can reduce conflict. The more we blend with the other person the less conflict there will be.

Blending with the other person can maximize similarities and minimize conflict.

We can do this by mirroring their body language, not mimicking it but gently matching it. We do this naturally when we are with friends. Just watch people in a café, restaurant or at a bar together and see how similar their body language is, or if they are not hitting it off how distanced and different it becomes.

So when you find yourself in conflict with someone, or disliking them, stop and ask yourself why this person is behaving in the manner they are? Even if you don't fully understand their reasons, or find them difficult to understand, this will at least prevent you from getting overemotional. Also remember that you can't change another person so it is no good thinking, 'I wish they would be more reasonable or compassionate, or understanding, or less hostile.' Wishing won't make it so.

To change a relationship requires persistence. Carol won't change her mother-in-law overnight. It will take her time and patience to change the relationship between them but she may have more success if she can understand her mother-in-law's personality.

Personality traits

So how can we get on someone's wavelength, even those whom we find it difficult to relate to? I always say to people, 'You think you're normal, but what is normal?' Normal is different to each and every one of us. We see the world through our own eyes, we think everyone should behave, act and be like us. Well of course they don't and they're not like us. We are all different. We all have different personalities and understanding this and recognising this can help us to adapt our approach to another person and get on their wavelength.

In 1926 William Marston came up with a model of Personality Types that is still used today. While people are highly complex and certainly more complex than the descriptions I am going to give you, this model will, I hope, help you to see yourself and others in a different light and enable you to change tactics to communicate more effectively.

We inherit personality traits from our parents, grandparents, great grandparents ... Of course this is influenced by other factors like upbringing, environment, education and levels of intellect and maturity but to make things more simple here we will look at the four basic types of personalities. Although we may contain a mixture of these traits some will be stronger than others within us. This dictates how we communicate and behave. See if you can recognize yourself from the descriptions below. Then think about how you might need to change your approach towards another person in order to influence and persuade them, and to manage them.

Type A – dominance

Type A personalities have dominance and superiority in their make up. This makes them rather impatient individuals. They are very direct people who 'speak as they find' and 'don't suffer fools gladly'. They are confident decision makers (although these may not always be the right decisions) but there is no pussy-footing around with these types. They are extremely time conscious and find it hard to relax. They are always doing something and even on holiday, if they take one, will want to be using the time 'wisely'. They can be rather intolerant of others who are slower than them. They manage or lead in an authoritative and often autocratic style, have a high degree of energy, and like getting things done. They are good at ideas, and at problem solving. They often enjoy going into troubled organizations to turn them around. They also often tend to be entrepreneurs, liking start up situations, being natural risk takers. They quickly get bored with the detail and are starters rather than finishers. When they get bored they will want to move on to a new challenge. Generally speaking they are high achievers and quite driven individuals pushing themselves onwards and upwards. They can take a high degree of stress, more in fact than other types, but there is a danger here in that they might not know when to take the foot off the gas. Because they drive themselves and find it difficult to relax they are candidates for burn-out and are prone to high blood pressure and heart attacks.

Type A personalities do not have a high need to be liked: *'If you don't like me then that's your look out'*, can be their response. Or you may hear phrases like, *'You have to be tough to do this job.' 'You can't make an omelette without breaking eggs', 'Getting paid to make tough decisions is what I'm here for'*.

Their influencing style is that of a tough battler, pressing for results, giving orders, issuing challenges, sometimes threats even. They are enterprising and forceful but can give the impression of being dictatorial and arrogant.

Managing a Type A personality

If you are managing someone who is Type A then ideally you should give them short-term goals, and projects that give them a high degree of recognition and status. Type As thrive on praise – often public, which is why many of them enter public life.

You need to ensure they have the opportunity to develop new skills and interest. Type As will often chase excitement and be thrill seeking. They don't like to depend on others and are in fact highly independent.

They are motivated by status, often favouring the status symbols, big and powerful cars, nice house, designer clothes. But status positions will also motivate them. They are competitive but not in a team way, competing against themselves and others to be better, faster, more successful.

They like to be in control and to feel that they have control over their lives.

Relating to a Type A personality

Two Type A's living together or married will find it very difficult. Because relationships are about compromise, two equally dominant individuals will find it hard to give in to the other. This will also happen within an organization if you have two Type A's vying for power.

When you talk to someone who is a Type A try and speed up the way you talk, be direct, get straight to the point and ensure that your handshake is firm and your body language positive. Don't go into too much detail. For example, don't go through a proposal step by step or they will quickly get bored and irritated and cut you short. Be clear, specific, brief and to the point. Use time efficiently and stick to the matter in hand.

How to recognize the Type A

From the description above you may already have a good idea of how to recognize a Dominant Type A personality. They will use dominant body language for a start (see page 64 for the kind of handshake you are likely to get.)

Their speech will be direct. They will not take time for social chitchat but will want to get right to the point. They will make flat assertions like 'That's rubbish.' They will also use a lot of 'I' statements and be ready to give you the benefit of their wisdom and provide advice on what you should do. Put a Type A in a group and you will quickly see them take control and lead that group.

If you were to ask them what sport they liked, or what their hobbies are, you will find that they enjoy single competitive sports rather than team games. Often Type A enjoys squash, golf, athletics and sometimes horseriding as handling an animal gives them a sense of control. They are unlikely to enjoy detailed pastimes like, for example, model making unless they have a high degree of Type D in their personality (see p.144 for description).

Type B – social

The Type B likes people and likes to be liked. They find it much easier than any of the other personality types to mirror and match another person's body language because they are more attuned to people needs and moods. They do it rather naturally because they want people to like them.

They are adaptable, flexible and participative. They have high energy levels and are articulate, confident and cooperative. They are enthusiastic, embracing and come up with lots of ideas and they are not afraid of change, in fact they thrive on it.

They are usually highly persuasive individuals who manage in a democratic style but find it hard to deal with confrontation. Because of their desire to please they can often change their mind to suit the person or situation, so can appear fickle and manipulative to some people.

Their influencing style is that of the friendly helper showing concern, expressing friendliness and warmth. They try to influence by appealing to others' emotions. Their optimism is usually a major influencing factor but they may be gullible and impractical.

Managing a Type B

If you are managing a Type B individual then you will need to give them short to medium-term goals and a consistent management approach. They thrive on variety and like lots of things to do and to be involved with people. If they are not working or involved in people then they will become demotivated and unhappy. Continued rejection and disapproval will also demotivate them. They need praise and approval. They find regulations restrictive and like to work in an environment where they are allowed freedom to use their initiative. Because of their high levels of energy and enthusiasm they can sometimes come across as being overbearing. Lack of concentration at times and a tendency to disregard rules means careful management.

Relating to Type B

You need to spend time building solid relationships with this person rather than simply issuing instructions. Leave plenty of time for socialising and take time to socialize at the beginning of an interview.

Appeal to their enthusiasm and their vision of things but be careful if you need to rein them in as you can dampen their enthusiasm and hurt them.

Recognising a Type B

You may still get the firm handshake but with this person you will have less dominant body language. Status is as important to the Type B as it is to the Type A so you could get the big car and the designer accessories but the essential difference between these two types of personalities is that the Type B will spend more time over the pleasantries, making you feel comfortable. They will not be so direct and forthright as the Type A. They will quickly participate in any meeting, throwing in ideas. They will be friendly, talkative and smile at you. Indeed you may have trouble shutting them up!

They enjoy team working and so their hobbies will often be people and team related, for example, football, netball and socializing.

Type C – measured

The Type C is measured and far more logical and analytical than either our A or our B personality. They are steady, often security minded and don't like a lot of change. They can be suspicious and sceptical of new ideas and it will take some time to persuade them.

They are consistent, caring and patient. They often make good nurses particularly if their C personality is combined with the people skills of a B Personality. They don't like taking risks and will only do so if they have weighed up all the pro's and con's. They are great list-makers!

Many engineers fall into this category, as they are attracted to the occupation by its analytical, methodical approach. Lawyers, accountants and professional buyers may also fall into this personality type.

Because of their cautious nature Type C's can have a tendency to procrastinate and over-plan. They are generally warm hearted but when aggressive can be very stubborn and intransient.

Their influencing style is based on logic and facts. Fairness is paramount to a Type C personality.

Managing a Type C

If you are managing a Type C personality then it is best to set long-term goals with careful and periodic reviews. The Type C needs to be told what you want; they prefer to rely on more assertive people to take the lead.

When introducing change it is best to do it in stages, introducing an element of trial and give them time to adapt. Explain and delegate with detail. Once embarked on a task the C will want to concentrate on it, and doesn't like interruptions and distractions, or changing the goalposts half way along. They work slowly and thoroughly. For this person to communicate more confidently they need to feel they have your support and encouragement. In informal or antagonistic situations they could clam up.

Relating to a Type C

In order to communicate more effectively with a Type C personality you should try winning them over with a logical reasoned approach rather than appealing to ideals which would succeed with our Type B or vanity or ego which would succeed with our Type A. Once you have won them over, or got a commitment from them, they are often very loyal and reliable. You need to take time to build relationships with them, giving them time to explore their real feelings.

Your open questions are vital here. These are people who will simply give you a one-word answer if you ask a closed question. They won't help you out like the Type B who could talk until the cows come home.

You will need to be sincere and show a genuine interest in them. Take time to find areas of common ground. Be honest and open and patiently draw them out in a non-threatening manner. Slow down, move casually and informally. Provide lots of assurances and give clear specific solutions with maximum guarantees. Give them the detail. If you don't, they will ask for it. You can't fob them off. Don't rush them – they don't like it.

For a Type A this can be very hard to deal with but if you want to communicate more effectively with someone who is a Type C then you must make this effort. Equally if you are a Type C communicating with a Type A then learn to speed up, prepare what you have to away from any meeting and when in the meeting be as direct as you can.

I had a good example of this when running one of my

courses. The headteacher of a school who was a Type A personality told me that he was having difficulty getting on with his deputy head. The deputy headteacher told me that she was having difficulty getting on with her headteacher. It was apparent to me that she was a Type C personality. She liked detail and he didn't. I told her that for her next meeting with him she should prepare as thoroughly as she could outside the meeting and that when she went into the meeting she should give the headteacher short sharp answers and only the information he required, leaving out detailed explanations. This she did and reported back to me with the result that, after the meeting her headteacher said, *'That was the best meeting we've had.'* He felt it was a good meeting because she had communicated with him in the style he liked, understood and could respond to.

Whereas our Type B is optimistic and enthusiastic our Type C is pessimistic and cautious. This can cause frustration between the two different personality types but equally the two can complement one another and work and live very well together if they recognize their individual personalities and strengths. Type B can encourage Type C to 'lighten up' and take risks and a Type C can reign a Type B back in when he or she goes 'over the top'! Two Type C's in a relationship will also work well. It might not be fiery but it could be a long, loyal and comfortable relationship.

Recognising a Type C personality

They are not motivated by status so the designer accessories, big cars etc. will be missing. In addition, there will be no dominant body language; the handshake can be firm or weak. Their dead giveaway though (unless they are very skilled) is their facial expression and body language. The Type C will be looking at you rather sceptically. They will sit well back in their chair with their arms folded, not necessarily with hostility, but they will reserve judgment on you and what you are saying until they have weighed you up and decided whether or not they like you.

Their hobbies will be those that require more detail and patience – perhaps fishing, cross stitch, cake decorating.

Type D – compliant

The Type D likes to comply with the rules and regulations. This means that they are usually very systematic, precise, hyperefficient and bureaucratic. These people love facts and detail, the more the better.

They can often be shy and self-effacing unless they have a high degree of B in their personality. Equally they could need a great deal of assurance depending on their level of intellect. Their compliant nature means they can often be easily agreeing which makes it difficult for you to know exactly what they are really feeling and thinking. They need to feel completely sure of their position and of others' expectations.

They can give the impression of coldness and disinterest and will use rules, authority and logical argument to influence the actions of others. They have a tendency to correct errors and inaccuracies that others might consider insignificant.

Managing a Type D

If you are managing a Type D then they like long-term

goals fully negotiated. They like harmony and tend to avoid direct confrontation. They need a detailed brief and explanation of reasons before doing anything. They can often prevaricate and do not like taking risks. They are concerned with quality, and do not want to accept inferior work regardless of timescales so you will need to allow plenty of time for them to do things. You will also need to delegate very specifically. They can be surprisingly ambitious with lofty goals but an innate lack of assertiveness and unwillingness to become involved in confrontational situations can make it difficult for them to achieve their goals.

They are punctual and like punctuality in others. Coupled with a high intellect, these people are attracted to jobs like systems analysts, researchers, medical consultants, scientists.

Their influencing style is based on logic and facts often quoting authorities and rules and regulations. Their weakness can be rigidity and nitpicking.

Relating to a Type D

You will need to give them plenty of time to make up their mind but gently direct them. Be straightforward in your approach, stick to the business in hand and build credibility by listing the pros and cons to any suggestions you make. Reassure them that there won't be any surprises. Be realistic and accurate and provide solid, tangible, practical evidence. They need time to make any decisions.

Recognising a Type D

With this personality type you may get lowered eye contact and fidgeting mannerisms. There will be no dominant body language, in fact the body language is much more likely to be submissive. The handshake can be perfunctory and not terribly firm. Compliant individuals can often speak quietly and can be vague. Again, as with our Type C personality the Type D will enjoy complex hobbies requiring patience and detail.

There are, of course, many more complexities of personalities than I have given you here but I hope the above goes some way in helping you to understand that we are all different and because we are we need to accept that different approaches work with different people. Being aware of the different personalities, reading the body language and keeping an open mind so that you try and understand where the other person is coming from can all combine to help you relate to other people more effectively, and, hopefully, give you the ability to communicate with them more confidently.

In summary

- the more you have in common with someone, the easier it is to get along with them
- people buy people, so enhancing the likeability factor can help us to influence others
- to change a relationship requires patience, persistence and understanding
- we are all different, and understanding and recognizing different personalities can help us to adapt our approach and hence improve our relationships

---

13

Communicating with angry people

It is never very easy communicating with angry people and when we are faced with anger we often go on the defensive, understandably so because it feels like we are being attacked, verbally! Our instinct is to either lash out **(fight back)** or run away **(flight)**. Sometimes flight is the best option, distancing yourself before saying something you might regret later. Or if the angry person is coming at you with a knife, for example, then running away is decidedly the best option!

Getting angry with someone who is angry with you will only escalate the situation so it is best if you can deal with this as calmly and as assertively as possible.

Your inner voice is critical here. Instead of thinking *'How dare this person speak to me like this'*, which will only make you aggressive towards them, it is far better to tell yourself to keep calm, that you can handle it.

My own response to anger is to depersonalize it by thinking, *'Why is this person behaving like this? There must be a reason.'*

You need to keep an open mind as to what is causing that anger, trying to see it from the other person's viewpoint.

When someone is angry it is not usually you they are angry with but the situation. Something has happened to make them angry. You need to deal with it before it escalates into a personal attack.

Get the right body language and inner voice

Body language is critical here. Keep your posture as upright and open as possible, telling yourself, *'I can handle this, I can deal with this, I can keep calm.'* Take slow breaths. Keep your eye contact on the other person and lean towards them. This takes courage. Mirror the other person's body language if you can but obviously if they are waving a fist at you it is not advisable to mirror this! What I mean is that if they are standing you should stand too, if they are sitting then sit down.

What to do next

Once you have got your inner voice under control and your body language right, listen hard to what they are saying. When people are angry they do not always express themselves clearly, in fact they rarely do. They let off steam. Allow them to do this and don't interrupt them. Let them have their say. You can never reason with someone until they have worked their anger out. When they have said what they needed to say then you can start asking them questions but before you do this summarize what they have said, stating the position as they see it. This enables you to check that you have fully understood the situation and shows them that you have listened. Keep your voice assertive, i.e. steady and controlled, neither shouting nor mumbling.

For example:

'So what you're saying, Mr. Smith, is that we promised to come and see you on Thursday and after waiting in all day, no one turned up?'

'Yes, that's exactly what I'm saying. I had to take a whole day off work.'

Empathize if you need to and apologize if you or your organization is in the wrong.

'I do apologize Mr. Smith. I recognize how irritating and inconvenient that must have been for you. Now, let me take some details and sort this out for you. What is the order number?'

Here I have apologized and empathized with him (well who wouldn't?) and then asked him an open question to get the facts. By this time hopefully Mr. Smith is calming down.

Sometimes you can also de-escalate this situation by asking the angry person what action they would like you to take. This puts the initiative (and the solution) firmly back with them, sometimes taking them by surprise and catching them off guard.

The 7 Step approach to communicating with angry people

The key then to defusing these types of situations and handling them more confidently is as follows:

1. get the right inner voice
2. use the right body language
3. apply critical listening
4. summarize what the other person has said to check that you have properly understood the situation. (This also reassures them that you have actually listened to them)
5. apologize if necessary and empathize
6. ask open questions
7. tell them what you are going to do to resolve the problem

And finally do it!

But what if you're right and they are wrong?

If their grievance is unjustified i.e. they are in the wrong and you are in the right then you need to state that in an assertive manner. State where you stand but show you are interested in their opinion.

For example: *'I recognize you have strong feelings on this, Mary but I see it differently.'* Here you have also empathized to a degree by recognizing their feelings but you have balanced this with stating your viewpoint.

If the person still maintains his/her anger you may need to step up your assertiveness.

For example: *'I don't believe I have ignored you Mary but I'd like to hear why you feel I have.'*

If the aggression is maintained then step up your assertiveness again; increase the emphasis on your position.

For example: *'I see it differently.'*

Don't allow them to reinforce their beliefs about the situation if it is incorrect. Set them straight on what actually happened.

If aggression is still maintained and the person begins or continues to shout or swear at you, then you should use the consequence technique; for example: *'If you continue to shout in this way, Mary, I will ask you to leave.'*

If all your efforts have failed either cut off the interaction – you have warned them – or perhaps you can try putting aside the issue you are discussing or arguing about and focus on what causes these arguments.

For example: *'Look, over the past three months we've spent lot of time arguing about this. It isn't good for either of us so can we set the issue aside for a moment and talk about why we always end up having these long arguments?'*

Get them to take their focus off **positions** (who is right and who is wrong.) Have them examine **behaviour and motivations** to understand why the issue came up.

Perhaps you can you look at this difficult person in a different light through trying to understand what their motivations are for behaving as they do, as we examined in Chapter 2? Or perhaps you need to understand their personality as we looked at in Chapter 12, this might help us to try a different tactic to connect with them.

Whatever the reason for anger do try to keep calm and count to ten before replying, take a breath and try first to understand how the other person feels, where **they** are coming from, rather than focusing on how you feel.

We all respond to problems that cause us stress in different ways, in fact different things stress different people. What freaks me out might not necessarily freak you out. This is obvious if you look at the differences in personalities we examined in Chapter 12. So instead of saying to someone, *'I can't see why you're so upset/angry/hurt about this, it's nothing'*, learn to recognize and accept that we are all different. It may be nothing to you but to the other person it is 'something.'

How men communicate problems

Men and women react differently to problems that cause stress. A man's reaction is to withdraw within himself. He doesn't naturally confide but likes to examine the problem for himself, trying to resolve it in his mind, or ignore it in the hope that it might 'go away'. Women do the opposite.

When women have a problem they like to discuss it, often confiding in close friends or their partner. Remember what we discussed in Chapter 9: women ask *why* first. *'Why have I got this problem?'* Whereas men will say *'How can I solve this problem?'*

The worse thing a woman can do when a man has a problem and 'goes silent' is to try and probe and get the man to confide. This will only prompt him to withdraw even further and/or get hostile, often causing an argument.

A woman's instant reaction when a man 'goes silent' is *'What have I done wrong?'* or perhaps *'Why is this relationship going wrong?' 'Why won't he confide in me?'*

(There's that *why* word again.) It is a macho thing that men have to solve their own problems and they certainly don't want a woman solving it for them as it implies (in their minds anyway) weakness. Once the man has solved his problem he will then reveal what was bothering him. When this happens don't say, *'Why didn't you tell me; I could have helped you'*, because it will only upset/anger him. He didn't and doesn't want your help. To you he must appear strong. Women should remember that men need to be approved and the woman who wants to improve her relationship with her man should make sure she reminds him that she approves of him by thanking him for even the smallest tasks he undertakes. Irritating I know but by God does it work!

So when he falls silent leave him alone. Let him solve it himself, get on with something else, bide your time and once he's emerged from his cave simply smile, give him a hug and listen whilst he tells you what was bothering him.

How women communicate problems

And how can men help women when they have a problem? Again don't try and solve it for them. When women want to confide be there to listen and encourage and give it your full attention. Don't say things like *'Well if I was you, go back in there and tell them you're not having any of it.'* Or *'I don't know why you do that job. You're always moaning about it. Tell them to poke it.'* Yes, encourage her to 'talk through' the problem, (sorry chaps but you really do have to do this) and then prompt by asking good open questions as we discussed in Chapter 8. *'So, how do you feel about that?' ' What do you think might help you resolve this problem?'* Or simply offer up a glass of wine, a smile, nod and a very attentive ear.

And always remember:

> Seek first to understand and then be understood.

In summary

- get your inner voice right when communicating with angry people
- when someone is angry it is not usually you they are angry with but the situation
- keep your posture upright and open, maintain eye contact, stand if they are standing, sit if they are sitting
- listen to what they are saying, ask open questions to clarify and fully understand the situation, let them have their say
- apologize if necessary

Conclusion

Final checklist for communicating with more confidence

Finally then in order to communicate with more confidence let's pull together all the elements that are involved.

- accept full responsibility for communication
- accept you cannot change another person you can only change the way you behave and act which will change the response you get
- be aware of the values, attitudes, pressures and prejudices of others, they may not be the same as yours
- keep an open mind and try and see where the other person is coming from
- get a positive inner voice, silence the negative voice
- adopt and practise giving out confident body

language, the body is connected to the brain and will send positive signals back to the brain making you feel and therefore act more confidently

- make sure the impression you are giving out is the one you want to convey for the people you are seeing and the situation
- use colours in clothing to boost your confidence
- practise good questioning techniques, using open questions
- fine tune your listening skills using critical listening
- understand that not everyone is like you; try different ways of communicating with different personality types to see what response you receive.

and finally ...

use every situation to practice and sharpen your communication skills both socially and at work because after all, as the saying goes

> Practice makes perfect!